Writing Guidelines
for Education Students

Writing Guidelines
for Education Students

SECOND EDITION

Edited by Lisa Emerson

Australia • Brazil • Japan • Korea • Mexico • Singapore • Spain • United Kingdom • United States

Writing Guidelines for Education Students
2nd Edition
Lisa Emerson

Project editor: Chris Wyness
Publishing editor: Sharmian Firth
Cover design: Olga Lavecchia
Production controller: Carly Imrie

Any URLs contained in this publication
were checked for currency during the
production process. Note, however, that
the publisher cannot vouch for the ongoing
currency of URLs.

First published in 1995 by Dunmore Press

Printed in Australia by Ligare Book Printers.
5 6 7 8 9 10 12 11 10

For product information and technology assistance,
in Australia call 1300 790 853;
in New Zealand call 0508 635 766

For permission to use material from this text or product,
please email **aust.permissions@cengage.com**

**National Library of New Zealand Cataloguing-in-Publication
Data**
Writing guidelines for education students / edited by Lisa
Emerson. 2nd ed.
Includes bibliographical references.
Previous ed.: Palmerston North, N.Z.: Dunmore Press, 1997.
ISBN 978 0 17 013391 3
1. Teachers—Training of. 2. Report writing. I. Emerson, Lisa.
II. Title.
370.71—dc 22

Cengage Learning Australia
Level 7, 80 Dorcas Street
South Melbourne, Victoria Australia 3205

Cengage Learning New Zealand
Unit 4B Rosedale Office Park
331 Rosedale Road, Albany, North Shore 0632, NZ

For learning solutions, visit **cengage.com.au**

CONTENTS

1

INTRODUCTION

While at a university or college of education you will very often be assessed on the basis of your written work. The main purpose of this guide is to introduce you to writing assignments in an education course context.

Lecturers ask students to produce many different types of assignments. You may be familiar with writing essays from your school days but probably reports, case studies and literature reviews will be new tasks. These different formats allow you to develop different skills. Essays test your ability to construct a logical argument, usually about an abstract or theoretical issue. Reports and case studies require you to apply concepts and theoretical models to practical situations. Literature reviews develop your skills in understanding, organising and summarising what other academics have written on a particular topic.

These various formats are described in detail in the middle sections of this book. The earlier sections focus on the research and writing processes. The Appendices pursue more specialised aspects of writing assignments and should be used as reference material.

This book is intended as a guide. If any of your assignment requirements do not appear to fit the formats described here you should always consult your course controller, lecturer or tutor. Be flexible in your approach and be prepared to adapt your format to suit the specific requirements of different courses and teachers.

1.1 Assignment presentation

Procedures for presenting assignments are detailed in this section. Individual courses may have different procedures; always check the course outline or assignment directions for your specific courses. (For more detail on layout and presentation see Chapter 11, page 86.)

Professional appearance

Students often underestimate the value of presenting their work well; this is a mistake. The visual impact of your assignment does influence your marker's evaluation. You are undergoing professional training; and for this reason the person marking your assignment will expect you to produce work that would appear credible in the professional work environment. You do not want your writing to convey the impression that you are careless.

Do not fill the entire page solidly with print. Offset the print with lots of white space; your assignment will be easier to read and important points will stand out.

Print on one side of the page only.

The use of headings, sub-headings, tables, diagrams and graphs all provide means to improve the appearance of a written project. It is important to be consistent in the use of styles that you adopt within a report (see Chapter 11 and Appendix F, pages 86 and 127 on presentation of data and headings).

All assignments should have a title page.

1.2 Margin for marker's comments

Leave a 3 cm space along the left-hand margin of each page of your assignment. You will get more useful feedback if markers have room to respond as they are reading. The text should be one and a half or double spaced to provide additional room for editorial comments.

1.3 Typing your assignment

Most lecturers or tutors specify (in course outlines) that assignments must be typed. If you don't know how to use a computer, now is the time to learn! Most tertiary institutions have computer labs that are available to students. If you don't have your own computer, find out where to access one on campus. If you are a distance student, your local library or internet café may have facilities you can use.

1.4 Responsibility for taking a copy

There is always a risk of an assignment being lost. Make a copy of your work before handing one in for marking. Remember that flash drives are easily lost, so don't keep all your back-ups there. Store every assignment on your hard drive and on CD or disk. Without a copy, if your assignment should be misplaced, you will have to rewrite the assignment or forfeit the marks: the responsibility of making a copy is yours.

1.5 Correct use of English

Like the visual appearance of your work, the correctness of your grammar, word usage, punctuation and spelling will also influence your marker. In some courses a percentage of the mark is given for language use. For tertiary-level work you are expected to understand and apply the basic rules of English. If you have problems with writing you should consult reference books (from a library) on English grammar and style – or you could contact a support person on your campus.

Even if you have good English skills, you need to take the time to proof-read your work. Spelling and other types of careless mistakes distract the marker from your work and diminish their sense of your professionalism. You should own a good dictionary – and use it often.

1.6 Plagiarism (also known as copying other people's work)

Copying another person's ideas or words without acknowledgement (i.e. plagiarism) is a grave academic and legal offence. It is viewed very seriously and the penalties can be severe. Discuss your assignments with fellow students by all means, but the work you submit for marking must be your own. If you want to include someone else's work directly into your assignment, the author and original source of this work must be clearly shown and credited.

1.7 References

For many assignments you will consult articles, books and other published materials. The list of references you use in compiling your work should be attached to your assignment (see Chapter 12, page 89 for details on how this list should be formatted).

1.8 Handing in assignments

Most courses specify due dates for assignments. Buy yourself a wall planner and as soon as you are provided with these due dates, plot them all on your wall planner. Make sure you write the dates of all assignments for all your subjects on the wall planner so that you can plan for particularly demanding periods, such as the end of semester, when many assignments are due.

Use a wall planner, even if you are also using a planning tool on your computer – the visual impact of a wall planner is invaluable. If you do use a computer planner, don't get carried away with perfecting your system – it can be a great form of procrastination! Try not to fall behind with your assignments. Some lecturers or tutors don't accept late assignments and others take off a percentage of the mark for work submitted late. But even if no penalty exists for late assignments, you need to pace your work so that you do not fall behind with other subjects.

2

FINDING INFORMATION

As an education student writing an assignment, you have a vast, and often overwhelming, amount of information available to you. Your course itself, for example, is made up of lectures, study guides and set texts. Additional material can range from in-depth scholarly research findings in books and journals to newspaper articles, a television documentary or a search on the Internet. On top of this, the sheer quantity of information makes it difficult to identify what is truly of value and to keep track of what you have found. Acquiring good information habits and skills as a student will not only improve your academic performance but will also lay a sound basis for your future career as an educator.

2.1 An information strategy

Start by clarifying your understanding of the topic and the information you will need:
- Do you understand all the terms used in the assignment question?
- Can you break the topic down into parts – what are the major concepts?
- What do you already know about the topic?
- What level of detail does your assignment require? Is it a brief class presentation or a research paper with a bibliography and footnotes?
- Do you need a general discussion of the issue, an understanding of theory and ideas or a list of facts, resources and statistics?
- Does your topic require historical information, material from the recent past or current data?
- Has your lecturer suggested that you consult certain types of materials such as popular or scholarly journals, newspapers or a particular database?

Begin with some background reading. Useful first sources would be specialist encyclopedias and dictionaries that will define terms and major concepts. They should also alert you to the existence of differing viewpoints where there is debate about a topic. Note down any relevant words or phrases that are used, and any references you might wish to follow up later.

Once you have done this, check your library's catalogue for books. Be aware that you possibly won't get an entire book devoted to your exact topic, so you might want to search for titles on the broad subject rather than on your specific focus. Remember too, that a single book on the subject will only give the views of its author(s) and you should probably supplement the information using other sources. The references at the end of a book are valuable guides to more information.

As you locate information, note down the sources you have found including publication details, page numbers, important passages and so on. This will allow you to accurately reference material when you come to write your assignment.

Once you have gathered the information (and read at least some of it) you can decide what is likely to be most useful for your assignment. Discard anything that is irrelevant. Any material that is aimed at a general audience needs to be treated with caution unless it is quoting actual research. Look at the remaining information you have found. Do the views presented in some of the books or articles contradict those found in others? If more recent work differs markedly from older research you are probably looking at a field that is changing over time and you should make sure you have a good representation of recent material. Most areas of research are marked by differences of opinion between experts and you may need to take more than one approach into account.

2.2 Sources of information

Encyclopedias and dictionaries

Many of the information sources you find will require some existing level of academic knowledge. Before searching for books or articles, consult specialist encyclopedias, dictionaries and handbooks to gain a basic understanding of the field. Some reference books will have articles written by specialists who can be relied upon to give an authoritative account of their subjects.

ADVANTAGES OF REFERENCE BOOKS:

- You can save time by ensuring that you understand key terms and concepts.
- You can acquire a broad understanding of your subject.
- You can quickly find out who are the key authors in a field.
- You have a good source of facts.
- Many online encyclopedias are regularly updated.

DISADVANTAGES:
- Reference books can be quite dated.
- It can be difficult to find the right reference book for your topic.
- With some general titles the coverage can be quite superficial.

Books

In many circumstances, books will be your most useful source of information. Their extended treatment can give you essential information and plenty of explanation. Most introductory texts will be written by one or more authors, whereas for a more advanced treatment of the topic you may need to find an edited book where each chapter is written by a subject expert.

Find books using your library's catalogue, which lists the author, title and publishing details of each book and also subjects, keywords and even chapter headings. Most libraries hold classes for students on how to use their catalogue, so don't hesitate to ask a librarian for help.

ADVANTAGES OF BOOKS:
- They can give you lots of information about the topic from one source.
- They are a good starting point that will give you an overview of your topic.
- You can use the index to find quite specific information.
- You can read them on the bus, or wherever.

DISADVANTAGES:
- They tend not to be 'cutting edge' as they take time to write and publish.
- Often it's more difficult to track down very specific information in books because they are not indexed electronically.
- Only one person can read them at a time and the one you want could be out on loan!

Conference papers

Academics often present their findings as a conference paper, a written version of the conference presentation. Conference papers are often the most current material on a topic, but they can be hard to find within a published volume of proceedings. You may need to know the name of the conference. Check with your librarian on how to best use this resource.

Journal articles

In the academic and research world, journals (also referred to as periodicals or serials) are very important. Most academic research is formally reported in the form of journal articles that describe the purpose of the study, the methods used, the results found and the conclusions drawn. These articles are written by experts for an expert audience and will assume that readers are already familiar with the topic. Journal articles tend to be written on very specific subjects.

Academic journals require a quality control process known as 'peer reviewing'. An article sent to the journal to be published will first be sent to one or more subject experts. They may reject the article or require changes prior to publication. By referring to peer-reviewed (or 'refereed') articles you help ensure that what you write is based on scrutinised material.

You normally locate journal articles by searching databases (see *Journal article databases*). Many researchers browse their favourite journals every month, but when you want to find specific information browsing is not effective. When you have identified an article you want, search the library catalogue by journal title to see whether your library owns it and holds that issue. The catalogue will only tell you if the library has the journal; not information about the articles. It is increasingly common for journals to be available electronically but even if you have accessed it online you should still reference it as if it were a print copy, quoting volumes, issues and page numbers. Whether the journal is electronic or print, your library catalogue should be the definitive list of what is available to you.

ADVANTAGES OF JOURNAL ARTICLES:
- Written and checked by experts.
- Very up-to-date in their coverage and include information that hasn't yet made it into books.
- Provide very detailed information.
- Written on a huge range of topics.

DISADVANTAGES:
- If the subject is a complex one you'll probably need quite a bit of prior knowledge.
- It can be hard to get an overview of the topic – articles can be quite narrow in their scope.
- You can be overwhelmed by the sheer amount of information.

To complete your assignment it may not be necessary to confine your research to academic, peer-reviewed journals. There are a large number of classroom resource magazines and professional development periodicals that will give you a pedagogical perspective or provide viewpoints on current practice. These types of publication may also be accessible via databases.

Journal article databases

Electronic databases contain references to articles from journals, newspapers and magazines and often contain, or at least link to, online full-text articles. However, you should be aware that a database may contain references to articles or journals that your library doesn't subscribe to.

ERIC (Education Resources Information Center) is the primary database for all aspects of education research and resources. Both AEI (Australian Education Index) and A+ Education cover journal articles, conference papers and some books on Australian education topics. APAIS (Australian Public Affairs Information Service) has excellent coverage of social issues including education. Index New Zealand (INNZ) is the most comprehensive database for New Zealand material.

ELECTRONIC DATABASE SEARCH TECHNIQUES:
- allow you to search the contents of thousands of journals at the one time
- find matches to your search terms anywhere in the references to articles, even if your word is halfway through a 300 word abstract
- look for matches using a complex set of terms
- use word truncation techniques to cover different endings of a word
- almost all use the same 'logic' in the way they put search terms together.

The Internet

The Internet is a fantastic information tool and is used daily by researchers, students, librarians and teachers all around the world.

Useful material you may be able to find freely on the web includes:
- government agency websites (often with education pages for teachers)
- statistics
- international academics' homepages with all their publications listed.

Do be aware that although there are vast stores of information on the Internet, searching the web is unpredictable. Your search may find items of real use alongside sites of little or no value. Not everything on the Internet is of good academic standard. Check the credentials of authors and publishers.

Because academic publishing is a business, a large proportion of the material you will need to use will not be accessible for free on the 'open web', so as well as using Google or similar search engines you must use your library's databases.

ADVANTAGES OF THE INTERNET ARE:

- It can be very up-to-date and give you access to cutting edge research.
- It can give you a quick basic overview of a field.
- It may give you access to specialised sources.

THERE ARE SOME DISADVANTAGES TOO:

- It can be hard to get beyond basic information.
- It can be difficult to trust the information you find.
- Websites change, move and disappear without warning.
- It can take time to sift, sort and select something truly useful.

2.3 Evaluation

As you locate information you also need to determine whether or not the book, article or website you have found is a good match to your information need.

Even when an item is relevant to your topic, it still needs to be understandable and valid, so evaluate what you have found carefully. Look at the publication date. If it was published decades ago it may no longer be relevant. Check the reputability of the material, the publisher and the authors. Where is the author employed? Do they regularly publish articles and books? Do other writers refer to their work? If there is a list of references at the end of chapters or articles, the authors are likely to have surveyed previous research and worked within academic guidelines.

2.4 Storing and using information

Many students and researchers use specialist software like EndNote, ProCite or Reference Manager to store their references and to output them in the appropriate bibliographic style. If you are struggling with recording information, or are undertaking a major project, it would be a good idea to check with your library to see if you can purchase a copy.

So now it is up to you to use the information you have discovered. Preparing a good research strategy will actually save you time by making your search more efficient and you will have less to read because you will only be looking at material of high relevance.

Finally, remember that the librarians in your institution are there to help you. If you are not sure how to do something or need advice on what to do next – ask!

A librarian is the student's equivalent of a Sherpa – an invaluable guide.

3

NOTE-TAKING

Generally students take notes when they attend lectures and when they are reading study material such as books, articles or Internet sources. There is no one correct approach to taking notes and individual students use different techniques depending on their personal learning styles, habits and experience. Students also focus on different aspects of a topic during a lecture and hence take notes that reflect these different interests. Note-taking style is highly personal and what is described here should be regarded as useful suggestions you can adapt and modify to your own personal situation.

3.1 Why take notes?

There are several reasons for taking notes. These include:
- preparing and revising for exams
- researching for assignments
- expanding knowledge in a field
- helping you to remember material
- organising thought processes
- achieving deep processing of information.

Perhaps the first four reasons are the most commonly given ones for taking notes. But what most people don't know is that if notes are carefully and systematically taken they enhance your ability to understand a subject at a much deeper and more complex level. And this is, after all, the aim of true learning.

3.2 The relationship between note-taking and memory

Most students seem to know instinctively that taking notes helps their memory. But how does your memory actually work in relation to note-taking?

The key to improving memory is to interact with new material and to repeat it. Memory is located in the synaptic connection that occurs in the brain – very much like a charge of electricity. The more times this electrical connection is made, the stronger the connection becomes; hence the stronger the memory becomes.

This is why reviewing notes is so important. If information is reviewed within 24 hours of first learning, the chances of remembering it are increased substantially. A suggested review plan is:

- review within 24 hours
- review after one week
- review after one month
- review again in six months.

But it is the notes that should be reviewed and not the original material. The notes that you have made serve as a trace of your interaction with the material and enable you to remember. Notes remind you of your original responses to the material.

Another important principle concerning memory and note-taking is visualisation. Human beings have phenomenal visual memories. Consider how many people's faces you have stored in your memory. You may not remember names but you can instantly recognise a face you haven't seen for years among a crowd of strangers. Turning new material into something visual is a very powerful way of aiding learning, memory and understanding. And one way of doing this is by creating a concept-tree (covered later in this chapter) with new information. Writing notes in the margin of a textbook also works in a similar way by aiding visualisation. If your lecturer puts their notes on the class website, take the time to read the notes and summarise – otherwise you will not truly grasp the information.

3.3 What is the benefit of taking notes?

One of the most valuable things about taking notes is that it forces you to articulate the ideas that you are hearing or reading. In putting ideas into your own words you begin to understand them. After understanding comes memory. It is much easier to remember something that has meaning for you and that you understand. Therefore, when working through study material you should be making notes to begin the process of understanding, which will lead later to deep processing and better memory of the material.

Interaction with material is another way of helping your brain to remember because you make mental connections all the time. Do this by making notes in the margins of your study guides as well.

3.4 Steps to follow while taking notes

As mentioned above, different techniques of note-taking are appropriate for different purposes. Sometimes the most useful thing to do is to get an overview of a piece of writing. This is especially good if you are planning to take notes on an entire book. Even with short articles, gaining an overview can sometimes be of tremendous use.

The following steps can be used for taking good notes:

1. Wait

Sometimes it can be very useful to gain an overview of a reading or book before you begin taking notes. There are various ways you can do this and some examples are described below.

The reason for taking notes should be clear before the job is started. Are you taking notes at a lecture or from a textbook? Are the notes for an exam or for research? The answers to these questions will affect the method you use and the amount of detail you choose to include. One of the most important principles of good note-taking is flexibility; you should be able to take sketchy notes at times and detailed notes at other times. Only you will know which approach is more appropriate.

Never start writing immediately. Whether reading study material or listening to a lecture, you should first try to understand what is being said, and then simplify it in your own words. If your lecturer is putting detailed notes up on a whiteboard or PowerPoint slide, don't try to copy every word – listen to what they are saying, interpret the key ideas, and summarise the visual notes. The aim of taking notes is to arrive at understanding first and then make the information memorable/meaningful for your own brain.

Try to focus on key words or ideas. This is easier said than done. Sometimes learning about a new subject, which has lots of new jargon for example, can be overwhelming. Trying to extract the key words and ideas can seem like an impossible task. The best advice in this situation is to persevere. As you become more familiar with your subject area, and begin to feel less overwhelmed by so many new and unfamiliar terms, key words and ideas will become apparent. Unfortunately most students have to go through a learning curve first before they can begin to understand new concepts.

2. Identify

When attending a lecture, take down the name of the lecturer, the course details and the date. This will make it easier to manage your notes (and file them) later. Also, using the same size paper each time makes organising your notes easier.

If you are taking notes for an assignment, it is important to record where the information came from. You may want, at a later stage, to refer back to the original material for clarification or to cite or quote the material in your assignment. At the top of the page write down the date and publication information. Make a note of the title, author, publisher and date of publication (see Chapter 12 for more information on referencing).

3. Space

Give yourself plenty of space in your notes so that when you revise you can make additional notes. Three methods of note-taking are described in this chapter – the Linear, Princeton and Mind-Mapping systems. You will probably have developed a preferred system of note-taking, but it is sometimes useful to know different approaches that you could try. See Section 3.6 for more details on these systems.

Don't write too small; it will be hard to read later. If you are creating mind-maps, you might like to use A3 paper to give yourself plenty of space for pictures and diagrams.

4. Key points

If you have in mind at the outset a broad knowledge of what the article or book contains, you will be better able to isolate key points.

Except for taking down quotations (which must be done in full and absolutely accurately) you should not take down word for word what you read or hear. Many students make the mistake of writing down too much.

If you are in a lecture situation listen carefully to what is being said and then summarise briefly what you understand. If a lecture has been properly constructed this is not too difficult as lecturers tend to repeat important points or write them on a board.

When you are reading study material always try to understand a point first and then select key words to write down. Depending on the length of a paragraph, it is better to first grasp the meaning before taking anything down. As a rough guide, try to comprehend a few paragraphs (or a page of text) before making any notes.

A well constructed paragraph should contain the sense of the paragraph in the first sentence or two. Summarise that key idea.

5. Interact

Your own notes are the best means for developing opinions about what you are reading or hearing. When writing assignments students are often expected to express a personal opinion or evaluation. These ideas are formed during the reading and note-taking undertaken before writing the assignment. As you take notes you can make observations and note comparisons, interesting points, authorial attitudes, points of cross-reference or contradiction. The point of doing this is to engage with the ideas – and this in turn helps comprehension and memory.

Once the notes have been taken and organised, you can develop trigger words or mnemonics to help remember key points. If a text belongs to you, write summaries and key words, or perhaps even questions, in the margins.

The more interaction that can be incorporated into your learning, the more efficiently you will be able to learn. As suggested earlier, reviewing notes (another way of interacting) soon after first learning is one of the best ways to facilitate understanding and memory.

6. In a practical context

Sometimes you will be required to take notes in a practical context – in a classroom for example. Appendix B has more information on how you might record and order such information.

3.5 Gaining an overview of study material

As suggested earlier, an overview can help you process information, understand it, and remember it. When making notes on an entire book or an article, you can get an overview by scanning the material first so that you know what it contains.

If you are reading a book, examine the contents page, index, date of publication, and any diagrams. The date of publication is important because it discloses whether the book and its ideas are current. Scanning the introduction is also a good way to get a quick sense of what is covered in the book. You will be able to approach the reading and note-taking with a superficial understanding of what is contained in the book. In effect this will develop a framework of ideas in your mind onto which you can later pin key ideas. Articles can be overviewed by quickly scanning headings and subheadings.

A very economical way to take notes without reading every word is to read only the topic sentence of each paragraph. Usually the topic sentence contains a summary of the rest of the paragraph and it usually comes near the beginning of the paragraph. At most you will be reading the first one or two sentences of a paragraph. This method is very useful because you can use it if you need to check whether an article is useful, to refresh your memory on something already read, or gain a quick (yet surprisingly detailed) overview of an article before reading it in more depth. It's a skill worth trying!

3.6 Different approaches to taking notes

The three different methods of note-taking that we will examine are: the Linear (or logical outline) System, the Princeton Method and Mind-Mapping.

1. The *Linear System* is probably the most commonly used of all note-taking methods and is the best for certain types of information, e.g. detailed facts. A common error is that people take down too much information, rather than simple key words.

   To use this method subdivide your notes into paragraphs and sections, using indentations of varying depth. Indicate the subdivisions with headings, numbers and other symbols.

   The limitation with this method is that it may be difficult to organise or connect concepts in the notes, depending on the complexity of the subjects. Perhaps you might like to take notes like this and then later organise the ideas into a concept-tree.

   For example: Study Skills
   1. Note-taking
      1.1 Linear System
         (i)
         (ii)
      1.2 Princeton Method
         (i)
         (ii)
      1.3 Mind-Mapping
         (i)
         (ii)

2. The *Princeton Method* is very simple and gives you space for re-reading and responding to notes.

Divide your page into three columns. The first column is used for the heading and main points, and the second for the summary. The third column is really useful for reviewing your notes. Or you can note things you didn't recall, examples, your own personal comments or a summary of the middle column.

Headings, main points, etc.	Summary of the notes	Blank column to use for related ideas, examples or for making a brief summary

3. *Mind-Mapping* provides unexpected advantages. First, you have to organise your thoughts as you draw the mind maps, which is an excellent aid to memory. Second, mind-maps are visual and the chance of you being able to remember the visual elements (and the information) is greatly enhanced.

Making mind-maps is a great aid to learning but it does require an additional investment of time. Even if you don't want to take your initial notes using this method, there are several other ways to use it. You can use mind-maps to plan tasks, read and research, plan and write assignments, and to revise and plan for exams.

How to draw a mind-map

When you are drawing a mind-map you need to:
• Select a brief phrase (one or two words) and/or picture that describes the topic, e.g. study skills.
• Write this phrase or picture in the centre of a blank page.
• Draw branches out from the topic to represent the main ideas. Write these main ideas down at the end of the branch. Use only one or two key words, not whole sentences.
• Add further branches to these main ideas to break the idea down into finer detail.
• Indicate associations between separate branches by connecting lines.
• Use as much colour and as many symbols or pictures as possible.
• Give yourself plenty of space. Use A3 sheets of paper for very complex mind-maps.

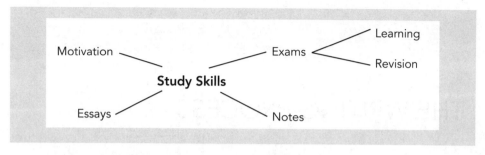

The note-taking method you use will depend on you and your subject area, but this skill is invaluable for tertiary study.

4

THE WRITING PROCESS

Novice writers tend to assume that writing an assignment has two stages: the first draft and the final copy. In fact, writing a major assignment should be a process that contains many stages. You should organise your time wisely to allow yourself sufficient time to do justice to each stage if you wish to achieve high grades. Everyone has their own approach to the writing process; this section outlines various stages that you may go through while writing an assignment.

4.1 What does the marker want you to do?

Carefully read the assignment topic and any directions given by your teacher. Most teachers design assignment questions for a specific purpose. Ask yourself the following questions:

- What format am I expected to use?
- Who am I writing for, i.e. who is my audience?
- What theoretical issues are relevant here?
- What is the exact practical application of this theory?

Make sure you are fully aware of what is required of you before you start gathering or analysing information; you may waste a lot of time if you don't attend to this first step.

4.2 Gathering Information

The nature and amount of information you will need depends on the requirements of the particular assignment. For some assignments the only material needed will be the notes you have taken on a placement or for a case study. Others will require extensive library research. For more detail on how to acquire information see Chapter 2, page 5.

If you are using published material, collect your material systematically – this will save you much time. The following method (adapted from Flower, 1985, page 229) is a useful procedure to follow:

- When consulting a book, Internet source or journal, write down the basic bibliographical information twice: with your notes, and somewhere apart from your notes and ideas.

    Cite: author
             title
             publication date
             publisher   } for books
             place of publication
             volume and issue number   –   for journals
             full URL and date of retrieval   –   for Internet sources

- Keep separate topics on separate pieces of paper or separate files so you can sort information later.
- If you quote from the text, quote exactly. To avoid unintentional plagiarism, indicate in your notes that this is an exact quote by using quotation marks ("…"). Note the page numbers or exact URL of direct quotations so that you don't have to wade through a book or article again if you decide to quote the passage in your assignment.
- Don't collect unnecessary data. Read critically, keeping your particular assignment task in mind and evaluating the relevance of the material to your topic as you read.
- Use appropriate materials. A Google search isn't going to help you produce an academic essay, for example.

Talk to your flatmates.

4.3 Generate your own ideas

You may choose to do this prior to gathering information. Either way, don't underestimate the ideas in your own head. Try brainstorming or free-writing (writing down all your thoughts on a topic without censoring them). Talk to anyone – classmates, flatmates, etc. – who will listen to you. You probably know more than you think you do about the particular topic, but you need to bring that knowledge up to the surface. Have confidence in your own ideas, thoughts and intelligence!

4.4 Drafting

Writing the first draft of an assignment is perhaps the most difficult, frustrating and, at times, surprisingly exhilarating part of the writing process.

Allow plenty of time for drafting. You are unlikely to write anything perfectly on the first try. You must write and rewrite. Fortunately, computers make the drafting and redrafting stage not so painful. Generally, the more drafts you do, the better the final version.

So, you have a pile of notes, statistics and printouts beside you and a clutter of ideas in your head. How do you organise it all? Karen Rhode, a writing teacher from Massey University's College of Education, identifies the following steps:
- Find a favourable location in a comfortable (and quiet) environment. Assemble your supplies. Make yourself inaccessible: the library, which is full of acquaintances and friends who may lure you into the student cafe, is not a good place for drafting.
- Slowly re-read all your notes, etc. Carefully review any outline made to guide the paper.
- Set aside your preliminary notes and write or type the draft as quickly as possible. Don't stop. If you are writing an assignment that is structured in sections (e.g. a case study or research report), start with the easiest sections. Don't re-read your writing.
- Don't worry about small mistakes or stylistic issues and don't linger over small problems. Concentrate on developing your ideas and working out your structure.

A note about 'blocking':

Everyone gets a mental block occasionally – indeed, some of us get them with alarming regularity! If you just don't know where to start, break the block by just writing anything that comes into your head and then gradually ease yourself into writing about the topic.

4.5 Revising

When you have finished your first draft you should always take a break so that you can come back to your manuscript and see it through fresh, and more detached, eyes: revision literally means to 're-see'. In the revision stage you should focus on the content and structure of your work – again, not on stylistic issues: look at the wood, not the trees.

Ask yourself the following questions:

- Have I done exactly what was required of me, i.e. does the content match the assignment requirements?
- Do my key ideas stand out clearly?
- Have I supported my key ideas sufficiently, i.e. have I provided enough evidence to convince my reader?
- Does the structure of my work highlight my key ideas?
- Would a different structure aid my reader's understanding?

Adopt the role of the reader; try to see your work through the eyes of someone else. Read through your paper, writing down the main points in each of the main sections to check the logic of the structure you have used. Reading your work out aloud (or getting someone to read it to you) may help even more.

4.6 Style

One of the issues to consider around revision and editing is whether you are writing in an appropriate academic style. Central to this issue is clarity. Generally speaking you are encouraged to write in a style which will be clear to your reader. Read your work aloud and think 'are these ideas coming across clearly? Will my reader understand me?' Use language that is appropriate to your particular course, but if you are finding the material difficult opt for short sentences and words that you fully understand. Writing in an academic style does not mean sounding stuffy and 'intellectual'; it means writing in a way that is understandable to the average reader.

Avoid qualifiers. These are words like *very, quite, really, perhaps, rather*. You don't need them: when you're editing your work, cut them out.

One tricky issue is whether to use 'I' in your writing. In the past, students were told never to use personal pronouns like this in their writing. In some subjects, e.g. most of the sciences, some social sciences and some business-related subjects, it would still not be appropriate to use 'I'. But some assignments will ask you for your own experience or for you to conduct research that involves your own point of view e.g. action research. The best advice we can give you is this: if you're not sure whether your lecturer or tutor wants you to include 'I' in your assignment, ask them. It's always better to check.

4.7 Editing

Editing refers to making changes to sentence structure and replacing words. Your focus should be on readability and style: now is the time to look at the trees rather than the wood.

You should be using a clear, uncluttered writing style to draw your reader's attention. Make each sentence clear and to the point, conveying its information in as few words as possible.

Check the following:

- Paragraphs   – Does each paragraph have a topic sentence?
  - Does each paragraph have a single subject?
  - Are your paragraphs a reasonable length?
- Sentences   – Are any sentences too long?
  - Have you written in complete sentences?
  - Have you varied your sentence length?
- Words   – How is your spelling? Use a dictionary!
  - Have you avoided slang and casual expressions?
  - Are there any unnecessary padding words that you could cut?
- Punctuation   – (See Appendix D, page 118)
- Referencing   – (See Chapter 12, page 89)

4.8 Proofreading and presentation

You should always, always proofread your final draft and adjust the presentation – however careful you have been, errors will creep in. Read your document through carefully for correctness – eliminate typographical errors, check your quotes and the little things such as page numbers, and whether your headings and numbering system follow a consistent format.

4.9 Hand in your assignment on time – and reward yourself

You deserve it!

5

FORMAL REPORTS

Education students may be required to write a formal 'business report' in the course of their degree or diploma. There is no single structure that can be applied to all reports; reports vary according to the needs of the person who requested the report, the context and the style of the author. You should be flexible when determining the structure of your report, taking each of these factors into account.

Writing a report to a client gives you practice applying theoretical concepts to a real life context. Learning to write a report, therefore, is not just a method by which your lecturers evaluate you; it is also part of your professional development, and a way of learning to communicate about real educational contexts and issues.

People professionally involved in education are required to write reports for a variety of audiences. Reporting to parents, caregivers or students is obviously an important task for teachers/educators in establishing a partnership between school or early childhood centres and home. Such reports are generally written in a format that is established by the school or centre. More complex reports about children, educational organisations or specific issues in education may, however, be required for other audiences, particularly when making claims for support or funding, or when trying to influence policy or decision-making.

Reports provide a basis for decision-making. They therefore require the author to exhibit investigative skills, judgement and the ability to write persuasively (Sligo, 1994). Writing persuasively for a report means you need to appear to be objective. You are required to produce proof or evidence to support your ideas. It is not enough to recommend a course of action; you need to explain why this is the best solution, what its short and long-term results will be, and explain the reasons.

Remember above all that a report is a practical project. A report assumes that someone needs to make a decision and they want guidance on how to make the best decision possible. If you are writing for a particular person, keep that person in your mind. Focus on that person's needs and recommend a solution that can be implemented. Be specific; avoid generalisations such as 'the school needs more funding'. Draw up an alternative funding scheme and show how it could be implemented and how it would solve the problems.

> **CAUTION**
> There are many ways of structuring reports. This section provides some basic guidelines for writing a report to a client. Always check with your lecturer or tutor for more specific guidelines. For details on how to write a research report see Chapter 9, page 64.

5.1 Basic report structure

The basic structure of a report contains six sections that are generally arranged as follows:

> Title page
> Introduction
> Discussion
> Conclusions
> (Recommendations)
> References

Figure 5.1: Basic report structure

5.2 Preliminary and supplementary sections

You may, in some contexts, be required to frame your basic report with some or all of the following preliminary and supplementary sections.

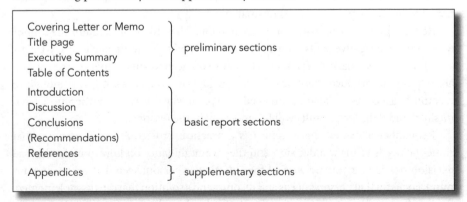

Figure 5.2: A report with all supplementary sections

These sections are used when the report may have a range of different readers. For example, if you are writing your report to a particular person, a covering letter or memo can be attached in front of the title page. An Executive Summary is designed for people who may not have the time to read the whole report but need to get a feel for the major findings. The Appendices are designed for the specialist reader who wants more detailed information than the average reader (for example, if the implementation of a new system for staffing schools is being recommended then the details of the system, which would be understood by a statistician or economist, could be placed in an appendix).

5.3 Report sections

The rest of this section describes the basic content of each section of a report. There are conventions relating to what goes into each section. The purpose of these conventions is to save the reader's time. If the reader just wants to know what your key findings are, for example, they do not have to flick through your whole report; they can turn immediately to the Executive Summary or Conclusions. If they want to know the purpose of the report, they can go straight to the Introduction. Use these pages, then, as a guide to mould each section. Be prepared to rewrite some sections until you are confident that the ideas have been conveyed clearly to your reader. If you are in doubt about the structure of the report, always consult the person who will read or mark it.

Remember that the purpose of your report is not just to complete your analysis. Reports are requested when someone has a particular need for specific information. Communicating your ideas, findings and the interpretation of results from analyses is vitally important. Express the ideas clearly and present them professionally.

1. Covering note: letter or memo

If the report is written by someone outside the organisation of the reader, a covering letter should be attached by the writer. If the report is for a reader within the same organisation as the writer, a memo is the appropriate format. The function of the covering note is to pass the report over officially from writer to reader. It reminds the reader(s) of the terms of reference agreed upon for the report, courteously acknowledges any assistance, and indicates the writer's willingness to supply more help.

Memorandum

TO: C N Spell

           C, ERO

FROM: Mr R Morris, Education Review Office

DATE: 19 August 2006

SUBJECT: Report on national truancy rates in primary
schools

As directed, I have completed an analysis of national truancy from primary schools in response to concerns raised by the Principals' Association.

I would like to thank the Principals and teaching staff involved for their co-operation.

Should you require any further analysis or wish to be provided with any additional information, please do not hesitate to contact me.

Figure 5.3: Format of a memorandum introducing a report

Aims of a covering note

The covering letter or memo should:

- identify the report topic, and scope or extent of investigation
- identify the person who authorised the report, and the date of authorisation
- acknowledge any assistance in preparation of the report
- indicate willingness to provide further information.

'Communication' South Regional Office
Cabel Street
DUNEDIN

19 August 2006

Ms Evert
Queen Elizabeth Primary School
DUNEDIN

Dear Ms Evert

Please find enclosed the report concerning national truancy rates in primary schools as commissioned by C N Spell, Chair of ERO on 1 July 2006.

I would like to thank the principals and teaching staff involved for their willingness to discuss issues of concern with me.

Should you require any further analysis or wish to be provided with any additional information, please do not hesitate to contact me.

Yours sincerely

Kaitlin Jones
Consultant

Figure 5.4: Format of a business letter introducing a report

2. Title page

The title page states the report's title. It should be focused and brief, but descriptive enough for the report to be filed appropriately. Position the title by itself about a third of the way down the page, surrounded by white space. Put the date the report was completed under the title. Place your name and the name of the person the report is being submitted to, with the paper name and number, in the bottom corner of the page.

Make your title specific and focused.

EXAMPLES

Poor: Streamed classes.

Better: Establishing a streamed elite class at Year 9 and 10 level at Queen Elizabeth College

3. Executive summary

Executive Summaries are being used increasingly in reports, especially reports to a wide audience. They reflect the likelihood that the report will have more than one reader, not all of whom are interested in the report's details. A useful summary condenses the essence of the report so that the reader can quickly grasp the report's aims, objectives and main findings (with key recommendations if the report is an action plan).

A common flaw in student summaries is the tendency to describe what the reader would find in the report, rather than to describe the report's highlights. For example, to say 'this report describes production difficulties, supply problems, etc.' does not inform the reader about these difficulties or problems. A better approach would be to name the key production difficulties and supply problems.

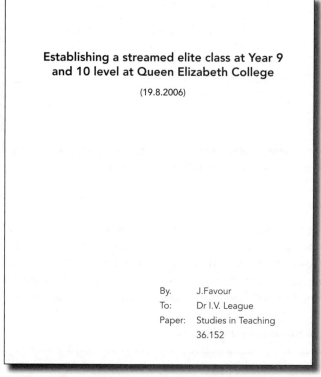

Establishing a streamed elite class at Year 9 and 10 level at Queen Elizabeth College

(19.8.2006)

By. J.Favour
To: Dr I.V. League
Paper: Studies in Teaching
36.152

Figure 5.5: Format of a title page

EXECUTIVE SUMMARY

The purpose of this report was to analyse the educational implications of establishing a streamed 'high ability' class at Year 9 and 10 levels at Queen Elizabeth College. Specific objectives were to identify both benefits and negative effects that such a structure has for students in the elite classes and students in 'normal' classes, and to offer recommendations to the school management for the following year.

Teaching staff identify some advantages for children in the high ability classes. However, the students themselves in these classes identify disadvantages associated with stereotyping and teacher expectations. There were also considerable disadvantages for students in the 'normal' classes. In addition, the identification of students with high ability was contentious and unreliable. The report recommends that the school discontinue streaming and adopt alternative approaches to extending and supporting students.

Figure 5.6: Example of an effective executive summary

4. Table of contents

If the report is longer than six pages, a Table of Contents helps to orient readers to the scope and emphases in the report. It also gives the page number for the beginning of each section. The headings of each section and sub-section should be identical to those that appear in the report. The logical relationship between the sections may be signalled by numbering, indentation or font size and upper/lower case, or a combination of these methods.

Table of Contents

Executive Summary	i
Table of Contents	iv
1. Introduction	1
2. Discussion	2
2.1 Defining ability and identifying high ability students	
2.2 Academic advantages for students in the high ability classes	
2.3 Disadvantages for students in high ability classes	
3. Conclusions	9
4. Recommendations	11
5. References	19
6. Appendix A: PAT scores of Year 9 students	21
7. Appendix B: Analysis of interview data	23
8. Appendix C: Ranked assessment data of students in different subject areas	26

Figure 5.7: A well-presented table of contents

5. Introduction

The Introduction should lead readers from information they already know and share with you, the writer, to information they need to acquire. Begin with a general overview statement that identifies the subject matter of the report and establishes common ground with the readers. Then state the change, problem or issue that has brought about the need for the investigation reported here. It is often helpful to present this 'change, problem or issue' in terms of a question that your report will help answer. In some situations it may be useful to state the terms of reference in the Introduction so that the reader knows the specific areas that are to be addressed in the report. Define the report's objectives precisely, and in terms that would interest your readers.

Having given the 'big picture', and then having focused on the issues to be explored in this report, do not keep readers in suspense. Your report is always written because someone has a question. Summarise very briefly your answer to the question addressed by this report. The next section will expand your conclusions in more detail.

Besides introducing the issues your report will discuss, this section should also clarify what readers can expect from the report. Indicate the scope of the report unless this has been done in a covering letter or memo. If evaluation or judgement is involved, set out your criteria for evaluating alternatives. It is also good practice to preview the report's structure, indicating how the material is grouped and in what sequence it will be presented.

In the world of business, report writers frequently comment in the report on its limitations. Even though you are writing as a student, it may occasionally be appropriate to caution readers about the variables affecting the conclusions and recommendations, for example, limited information, or assumptions that you had to make.

1. Introduction

This report was commissioned by the Board of Trustees at Queen Elizabeth College. Its purpose is to analyse and advise on whether the school should continue its current policy of running a streamed high ability class at Year 9 and 10 levels.

The identification of 'high ability' children has always been an issue of contention at the school, with concerns that children were often inappropriately placed in either high ability or normal classes. The concept of high ability streaming has also been contentious both within the school community and the education literature. Staff, students and parents have voiced considerable criticism of the policy in recent years. Their concerns over the educational implications for students in normal classes are also reflected in the literature on streaming.

This report analyses the issues involved in streaming at Queen Elizabeth College and recommends that the policy be discontinued. The report recommends a variety of alternative approaches to recognising, supporting and extending talent, creativity and ability.

Figure 5.8: Example of a good introduction

<table>
<tr><td>

WRITING AN INTRODUCTION

The Introduction should:

- briefly describe purpose and context
- identify the general subject matter and context
- describe the change, problem or issue to be reported on
- define the specific objectives for this report
- indicate the overall answer to the query explored in the report
- outline the scope of the report (extent of investigation)
- preview the report structure
- comment on the limitations of this report and any assumptions made.

</td></tr>
</table>

6. Discussion

This is the main body of the report. Normally it will take between 2/3 – 3/4 of your word length. It should be subdivided into logical units, each with an informative heading and a number. (See Chapter 11, Editorial Style, page 86 for more detail on presentation.)

The discussion of a report has two main purposes:

- to explain, in full, your conclusions; and
- to justify your recommendations.

Your conclusions and recommendations merely identify your findings and solutions; in the discussion you explain why you identified certain issues as important or problematic and why one solution is preferred rather than other possibilities. Show what the long-term effects of the problems will be if the situation remains as is, and what the short-term and long-term benefits accruing from the recommendations will be.

Remember that it is important to back up your claims with evidence from the case or situation. Support your analysis with practical observations and/or with theoretical evidence: link theory to practical issues. Explain practical effects in terms of appropriate theory. Use theory to give weight to your practical analysis.

It is important to persuade readers of the validity of your stance. If they are going to make a decision on the basis of your analysis, then they have to be persuaded that your ideas have value, that they are relevant and practicable. Keep your reader clearly in your mind and explain each step of your analysis as you go – take your audience with you.

Present your analysis in a logical, systematic way and divide the material with appropriate headings to ease the reader's understanding.

2.1 Defining ability and identifying high ability students

The definition and assessment of ability has been the focus of educational contention for decades. Despite this, the use of psychological testing to classify and stream children in terms of ability level in secondary schools went largely unchallenged in this country until the 1990s (Olssen, 1998). Since then, however, there has been considerable academic and public debate about the validity of unitary concepts of intelligence or ability and what is actually being measured by tests such as TOSCA, PAT, and OTIS (Nash, 1998).

In the past decade the debate about 'ability' has taken a new direction as a result of concern that education has not been meeting the needs of gifted and talented children. This debate has been very productive in highlighting the particular needs of gifted and talented children. However, at Queen Elizabeth College there is no shared understanding amongst the school community regarding the concept of ability and related concepts such as creativity and giftedness. Given this confusion, the identification of appropriate approaches to assessing children's ability is, not surprisingly, an area of considerable argument and concern.

2.2 Definitions of ability and intelligence

The debate about ability and intelligence is compounded by the prevalence, amongst all members of the Queen Elizabeth College community, of common-sense notions of ability, brightness, cleverness and intelligence. Such common-sense understandings often implicitly assume a unitary or generalised underlying trait. However, despite considerable research, there is no clear evidence that any single such trait exists (Bourne and Moon, 2004). The tendency of recent research has been to indicate that how well a child performs in any particular activity or task is dependent on a considerable range of intrapersonal, interpersonal and contextual variables (McInerney & McInerney, 2005).

At Queen Elizabeth College, this variability in 'ability' in different contexts is clearly evidenced in the experience of children in the high ability group. One child, for example, explained that 'just because I'm good at English, they assume that I'm going to be OK in science, and then you feel really stupid if you want to ask a question' (pers. comm.).

2.3 The use of psychological testing

The use of psychological testing as a basis for streaming children is widespread both in Australasia and overseas (Moon & Mayes, 2004; Olssen, 1998). However, over the last few years at Queen Elizabeth College, teachers and parents have questioned the fairness of testing as a basis for placing children in the high ability group.

Figure 5.9: Example of an effective discussion section

Research supports these concerns and it has indicated that streaming consistently places children who are in lower SES groups and children whose date of birth makes them relatively young for a particular year group in lower streams. The disadvantage that stems from this is frequently compounded by a tendency for younger, less experienced teachers being given low status lower stream classes (Bourne and Moon, 2004). In this country, a particular concern is that such tests discriminate against indigenous children (Nash, 2003).

2.4 Other methods of assessing ability

Over the past two years at Queen Elizabeth College, there has been an attempt to use a variety of other information in assessing children's ability. A particular area of concern here is that such assessment has been particularly unreliable with different teachers and feeder schools using a variety of approaches that lack both rigour and consistency

The issue of assessment is taken up in the Recommendations of this report. Assessment is clearly foundational to ensuring that the learning needs of children with special abilities (and indeed all children) are appropriately catered for within schools.

Figure 5.9 (continued): Example of an effective discussion section

7. Conclusions

The Conclusions section of a report summarises the key findings of the report in the Discussion. It must be grounded in the present situation. The key findings are presented as a list of numbered points that highlight crucial problem areas or issues to be considered by the reader. The Conclusions should relate directly to the objectives or terms of reference laid out in the Introduction.

WRITING A CONCLUSIONS SECTION

The Conclusions should:

* relate specifically to the objectives for the report set out in the Introduction
* be a list of numbered points
* follow logically from the facts in the Discussion
* be clear-cut and specific
* be arranged so that the major conclusions come first
* be short (full explanation is given in the Discussion section)
* identify the major issues relating to the case.

8. Recommendations

While Conclusions are grounded in the present situation, the Recommendations focus towards the future. Recommendations are the subjective opinions of the writer about what course of action should be followed. But subjectivity does not mean anything goes. Recommendations should take into account such issues as cost, location and acceptability relative to current policy or practice.

The reader should also be prepared for the Recommendations by material presented in the Discussion section. They should not come 'out of the blue'.

Note that not all reports have Recommendations. They are only included in reports that aim to specify a course of action. At least some of them should be immediately actionable.

---

3. Conclusions

3.1   There are very few educational advantages to be obtained from having high ability groups in years 9 and 10 at Queen Elizabeth College.

3.2   The selection of students for the high ability group is contentious and disadvantages particular groups of students.

3.3   Students in the high ability group do not have a full opportunity to work collaboratively with students with a wide range of abilities in different areas of the school curriculum. Students in the high ability group are disadvantaged by stereotyping and are sometimes pushed into narrowly 'academic' areas of study.

3.4   Children in 'normal' classes are also too often disadvantaged by stereotyping and self and teacher expectations. This appears to be particularly detrimental in the case of children whose close friends are placed in the high ability class.

3.5   More appropriate and equitable approaches to recognising, supporting and extending talent, creativity and ability are available to Queen Elizabeth College.

Figure 5.10: A conclusions section

4. Recommendations

4.1 The high ability classes should be disbanded at the end of the current year and full mixed-ability classes should be used in these year groups.

4.2 An assessment committee should be set up immediately with responsibility for revising the school's assessment policy and practices. Particular attention will need to be given to appropriate methods of assessing talent and creativity in different curriculum areas and in the essential skills. Responsibility for establishing this committee should be undertaken by the deputy principal.

4.3 An initial program of staff development in catering for children who are gifted and talented should be set up in the latter part of the current year. Networks already exist with the University College of Education and they have indicated their willingness to become involved in staff and school development. Two staff members at Queen Elizabeth College are already undertaking distance education study in this area. The Dean of Year should undertake responsibility for coordinating this program.

4.4 One area of school and curriculum development for the following year should focus on developing innovative responses to the needs of gifted and talented children at Queen Elizabeth College. This should be coordinated by the Dean of Year.

Figure 5.11: Example of an effective recommendations section

WRITING RECOMMENDATIONS

Recommendations should be:

- action oriented
- feasible
- related logically to the Discussion and Conclusions
- numbered (where there are several Recommendations)
- arranged in order of importance
- brief.

9. References

Every report you write that draws on other people's ideas or findings must have a Reference section where all sources are cited in full. It is common practice to use APA referencing for all assignments. (See Chapter 12, APA Referencing, page 89)

The purpose of the Reference section is to list all the sources you have cited in your report. If sources have been used but not cited, they should not appear in your Reference section. If there are sources that have been influential but not cited, they should be listed under the heading Bibliography immediately following the list of references.

10. Appendices

Material that is complex and/or detailed is collected at the end of the report in the Appendices section so as not to distract readers from the main theme.

Appendices may contain supplementary illustrative material that your readers may want to refer to after they have read the report, such as questionnaires, letters or pamphlets, which illustrate some aspects of the material you discuss in your text.

Appendices are also useful to locate detailed explanations of a model or theoretical approach referred to in the discussion. If some specialist readers – but not most readers – would want certain material, it should be placed in an appendix.

Appendices should always be presented in a professional manner, so do not be tempted to just fold up all your computer print-out figures and staple them to the end of the report! The material still needs to be organised and presented in a way that is easily understood by your reader. Appendices should always be given a number or letter, and title:

Appendix A: PAT scores of students in Years 9 and 10

or Appendix 1:   Analysis of interview data

When referring to an appendix in the body of your report, explain its significance. Do not just add 'Refer to Appendices 1, 3 and 7' to the end of a sentence. Rather, explain to the reader how the appendix will be of use to them with a sentence like 'Refer to Appendix A for a more detailed description of this model'.

WRITING APPENDICES

Appendices should:
- provide detailed explanation serving the needs of some specialised readers
- be clearly and neatly set out
- be numbered (or lettered)
- be given a title
- be arranged in the order that they are mentioned in the text
- be related to the report's objectives and not just 'tacked on'
- be listed in the Table of Contents.

11. Presenting your report

The following points should be used to guide the presentation and style of your report.

PRESENTATION ISSUES

- Start all new sections (but not sub-sections) on a new page.
- Use a numbering system to structure your work. Present your work professionally, using plenty of white space.
- Use double line spacing between paragraphs rather than indenting the first line of each paragraph.

5.4 Revision checklist: Reports

Key question: Have I answered my objectives?

Covering note:	Do I need to include a covering note?
	Have I used the appropriate format?
	Is it professionally presented?
Title page:	Is my title brief and descriptive?
	Have I formatted this page correctly?
Executive summary:	Is an executive summary required?
	Does my executive summary stand alone (i.e. without referring to the report)?
	Does it outline the key objectives and findings?
Table of contents:	Is a table of contents required (i.e. is the report 2000 words or more)?

	Is it formatted professionally?
	Have I used an appropriate numbering system, and descriptive headings?
Introduction:	Have I included: context, purpose and objectives, major findings, and limitations and assumptions?
Conclusions:	Have I listed my key findings in order of importance?
	Are my conclusions grounded in the present?
Recommendations:	Are they: practicable, action oriented, specific and clear?
Discussion:	Have I fully analysed the present context?
	Have I prepared the ground for my recommendations?
	Have I supported my analysis with appropriate theory?
	Have I divided my discussion into useful sub-sections?
References:	Are my references listed according to APA style?
	Is the list complete?
Appendices:	Has each appendix been given a clear title and numbered?
Style:	Have I written in a style that is accessible to my audience?
	Have I written with my reader's needs in mind?
	Have I explained theoretical terms?
	Have I proof-read my work carefully?
Presentation:	Is my report professionally presented?

6

ESSAYS

Essays are commonly used for assessment purposes in education. You will be required to write essays as part of your internal assessment and in exam situations. This section of the Writing Guidelines considers essays in general. If you are preparing for exam essays, you should read both this section and Appendix F, page 137: Exam Skills.

Essays require some very specific skills. They require you to acquire and assess a range of information in the light of a particular question. This means that you need to distinguish between different sorts of information, evaluate what others have said and then formulate your own ideas in the context of these different perspectives. Finally, you need to be able to present your ideas in such a way that your reader knows that you understand the debate on a particular topic and that you can logically present a case for a specific perspective on the topic.

6.1 Essay structure

Essays have a remarkably simple structure compared with reports. In English teachers' jargon, the structure of an essay is the statement and logical defence of a proposition. Put more simply, this means that an essay states a key point – or series of points (a proposition) – in its introduction. The body of the essay then explains why these key points are true and just, i.e. What evidence supports your point? It may also consider why the opposing position(s) is weak. What figures, facts, ideas can be used to defend this perspective? Then at the end, the essay summarises the main supporting evidence and restates the key point, the proposition. The diagram on the following page shows this basic structure.

Usually the essay is set out as a single unit without headings; however, you will invariably meet a lecturer or marker who likes headings. The general rule to follow is this:

Don't use headings in essays unless you have been specifically instructed to do so by a teacher. If in doubt, ask your lecturer or tutor.

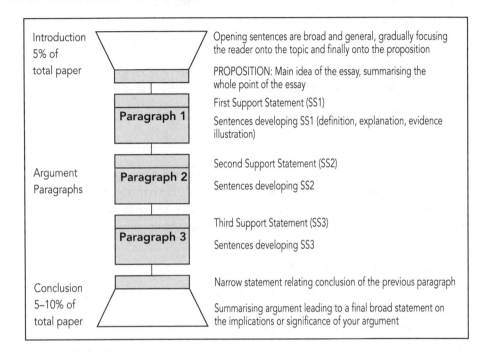

Figure 6.1: Basic essay structure

I. Introduction

Introductions usually start with broad and general statements about the topic and become gradually more focused until you state your key points at the end of the Introduction. You might begin with some background information, a question, dilemma or paradox, or an eye-catching quotation. Avoid starting with dictionary definitions, a restatement of the topic or the utterly boring 'The purpose of this essay is to prove that ...'. Aim to draw your reader into the topic.

Remember, your key idea(s), your proposition, should be placed at the end of your introduction. An essay is not like a short story – it does not require a surprise ending. Your reader wants to know exactly what you are talking about.

2. Body

The body of your essay is made up of paragraphs. Each paragraph is a single building block in the construction of your essay and should contain a single idea. The key idea of each paragraph should be situated at the beginning of the paragraph (the topic sentence), with the rest of the paragraph supporting, defending and explaining that idea. (See page 118 for more on paragraphing.)

> Don't forget to consider all the evidence *against* your case. Explain why you have nevertheless decided to *support* your proposition.

3. Conclusions

Your conclusion should summarise your supporting evidence and restate your key point(s). It is often appropriate to widen your perspective in the final paragraph, showing how your study has implications for further research. However, do not introduce any new ideas at this stage – your conclusion's main purpose is to sum up.

6.2 The essay writing process

Figure 6.2 on page 48 shows two methods that can be used in writing essays.

1. Select the question you will answer

Where a choice of essay topics exists, review the topics and choose one well in advance of the due completion date. Take into consideration your interest in the topics given, and the relative ease/difficulty and potential usefulness of the questions (e.g. How important is this topic in the paper I am doing? Am I likely to get a question similar to this in the final exam?).

2. Question the question

Spend some time making sure that you comprehend the essay question you have chosen. Make sure to:

- be very clear on what the question requires
- analyse central terms and concepts to ensure that you know what you are supposed to do
- review what you already know of the topic and determine what you still have to know (it helps to write these down)

- identify important issues either stated or implied in the question
- anticipate and isolate side issues.

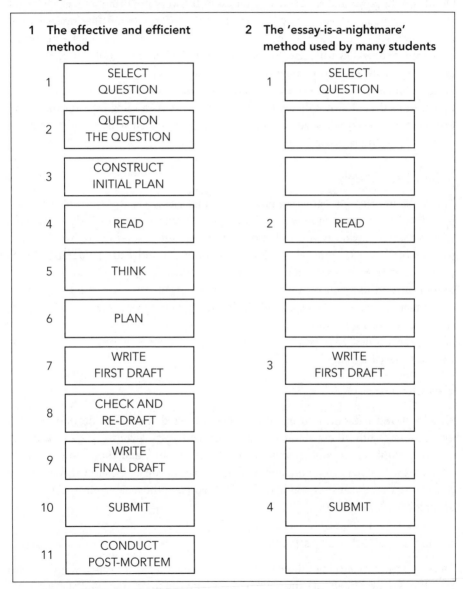

Figure 6.2: Basic steps in essay writing

3. Construct an initial essay plan

Decide on the scope and structure of your essay. It is very important to have planned the broad structure of your essay in advance of the information gathering (reading) phase. All that is necessary at this stage is a series of broad headings with some indication of how they will relate to one another in the final essay. (Of course, in some cases – especially where you know very little about the topic – it may be necessary to do some initial browsing beforehand.) From the plan you have constructed a series of questions should evolve that you can then use as your 'reading plan' for the essay. Reading for the essay will then be reading with a purpose – an active enquiry – rather than a passive and largely purposeless reading of material.

4. Read selectively

This is the information gathering phase. Read material relevant to your initial essay plan. (Where necessary modify your initial plan to take account of insights derived from reading.) Obviously you will also need to take notes, but do not rewrite whole sections of textbooks, journal articles, etc. Do *not* cut and paste paragraphs from electronic sources into your notes – you are in grave danger of plagiarism. Try to summarise and use your own words as much as possible (this will also help you to understand the material better). Write down only the points essential to your essay. If you need to use a quotation, copy it down accurately; its source will also need to be properly acknowledged in your essay. For more detailed methods of note-taking from written material see page 12.

5. Think

Stand back and assess the information you have gathered. If you have the opportunity to do so, talk with others about the ideas and concepts of your essay and reading material. Think about your overall answer to the question and about how you will integrate the facts, data, opinions and other information you have collected. Make sure you are clear on the answer you have decided upon and the major points you will be making. (See Figure 6.3.)

6. Plan a revised essay structure

An essay basically consists of three parts: the introduction (where you briefly describe what the essay will be about), the main body (where you make your points/ assertions backed by evidence), and the conclusion/summary (where you briefly sum up what the essay said and state any conclusions you drew from your study). It is very important at this stage that you make a detailed plan of the main body of your essay (the introduction and conclusion/summary can – if you wish – be sorted out and written at a later stage, when you're checking and re-drafting). The detailed plan should (ideally) consist of a paragraph-by-paragraph outline of the points/assertions you wish to make and their supporting evidence, explanations and/or arguments. Making a detailed plan will greatly assist you in the writing stage to be focused and less likely to lose the direction or logic of your essay.

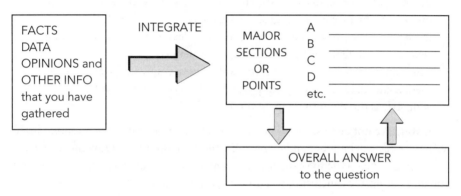

Figure 6.3: Essay plan

7. Write the First Draft

Using the plan you have made, write a draft essay that analyses, synthesises and evaluates your ideas on the topic. Try to express your ideas as clearly as possible. As a general rule, for example, the first sentence of a paragraph should convey the main point you want to express in that paragraph. The following sentences should then elaborate on, support, explain and/or argue for that point. If you encounter the problem of finding it difficult or 'impossible' to write down the thoughts you have: first clarify in your mind the specific point you want to make, then think aloud or vocalise your ideas – as if you were explaining or relating it to someone else. Once it 'sounds' clear enough to you, write it down; once written down, you can then improve the sentence structure if necessary. However, try to avoid perfectionism: remember that this is just your first draft and at this stage the most important thing is that you manage to write down and organise your ideas on paper.

8. Check and re-draft

After you have written the first draft of your essay, leave it for a day (if you have the time to spare) or overnight – so that you can examine it from a fresh perspective during the checking and re-drafting stage. Edit the essay for irrelevancy, excessive length, and faulty logic or grammar. Make sure that:

- you have kept to the topic, answered the question given, and excluded irrelevant points and unnecessary padding
- the main ideas or points are distinguished in separate sections
- the sub-topics are connected in sequence logically
- the sentence structure is logical, grammatical, clear and easy to understand
- central and contentious terms are adequately defined
- your argument is logical and directly addresses the question given
- there is adequate evidence to support your claims or generalisations
- your style is not too heavy, repetitious or dull.

If you have not done so yet, write the introduction of your essay, outlining briefly what the essay will be about and mentioning the main points or arguments you will be making. And then write the conclusion/summary, briefly summing up what the essay said and stating any conclusion you drew from your study.

9. Write the final draft

Most lecturers no longer accept hand-written essays or assignments; so, if you have been handwriting your drafts, type up your assignment. Always make sure you are familiar with and comply with the documentation and format requirements of your department and lecturers.

10. Submit the essay

Make sure you provide clear identification of the assignment, paper, your name and other requested information on the cover page.

11. Conduct a post-mortem on the essay

When the essay has been marked and returned to you, consider the marker's comments (if there are any). Note the good points (and errors) you have made. Make an effort to learn from the feedback you receive to gain a better understanding of the concepts/ideas/issues involved, and to improve on subsequent essays. If necessary make an appointment to see your marker/lecturer/tutor to discuss and/or clarify points in the essay.

Essay checklist

1. Is my opening interesting?   Yes/No

2. Do I have a clear proposition?   Yes/No

3. Is the proposition at the end of the introduction?   Yes/No

4. Do my paragraphs have topic sentences?   Yes/No

5. Have I used effective transitions?   Yes/No

6. Have I used in-text references to support my ideas?   Yes/No

7. Is my conclusion clear and effective?   Yes/No

8. Have I missed any key ideas?   Yes/No

9. Is my reference list formatted correctly?   Yes/No

10. Have I used clear sentences and eliminated clutter?   Yes/No

11. Have I proof-read my work?   Yes/No

7

RESEARCH PROPOSALS

7.1 Purpose

The purposes of an academic research proposal are:
1. To provide sufficient information to enable the reader to evaluate:
    - the merit of the proposed research
    - the appropriateness of the proposed research methods
    - the adequacy of the research design
    - whether the project is realistic and feasible in terms of time and funding requirements.
2. To provide the reader with a clear indication of what the researcher is expecting to do, how, when, why and at what cost.

And as the research proposal is an important means of obtaining funding, it must be more than merely informative; it must be persuasive, in the sense that it must be well written, professionally presented and clearly laid out.

7.2 Organisation

A typical research proposal comprises the following sections:
Title page
Background
Objectives
Literature review
Method
Ethical considerations
Budget
Timetable
References

7.3 Title page

The title page should convey the following information:
- the title of the proposed project
- the course number
- the name of the researcher
- the date of submission
- the name of the supervisors
- the name of the researcher's department.

7.4 Background

The background section should provide the context of the report and outline the problem under study. The information in this section is usually based on the review of the relevant literature, which you should have conducted prior to the writing of the proposal.

The background section should be concise, but detailed enough about the context so the reader will clearly see how the proposed research project relates to the broader body of knowledge, and gain an appreciation of the merits of the proposed research.

7.5 Objectives

The objectives of the research state what you are planning to investigate. They must be specific if the research is to be manageable and meaningful. Avoid vague statements of any kind. It is common to start with a broad, general objective, and then provide a series of smaller, more specific objectives that your research method will address directly.

Specifying the objectives allows the reader to judge the feasibility of the study. The objectives also provide you, as the researcher, with a very clear idea of what you are setting out to achieve.

A proposal should be persuasive.

7.6 Literature review

For many undergraduate research projects, the literature review is undertaken following the acceptance of the proposal, and is not required as part of the proposal itself. Indeed, the process of undertaking a literature search and review is often a major part of research exercises undertaken at undergraduate level.

However, for postgraduate research, a comprehensive review of the literature should be completed before the proposal is written, since the literature review may reveal that the topic under consideration has already been adequately researched.

The review will often assist you with the task of identifying suitable research objectives, and will often suggest appropriate research methods and identify methods that are not appropriate. Perhaps most importantly, the review will enable the researcher to place the study in context and will indicate how the study relates to previous work.

For more detail on how to write a literature review, see Chapter 8, page 59.

7.7 Method

A proposal for academic research should describe the method in detail, and this often includes a rationale for proposing a particular method.

The purpose of the method section is to describe how the study is to be conducted, and this should be described in sufficient detail to allow the reader to evaluate the proposed research design and method. The question your reader will be asking here is 'How effectively will the method address the research objectives?' For advanced-level quantitative studies, the method is typically reported under the following headings:

- Procedure
- Sample
- Instruments

However, most projects at undergraduate level would not require such headings, as long as the appropriate information is presented in a logical, concise and clearly written way. When these headings are not included, the information can be integrated to achieve clarity.

Procedure

The method section needs to explain what is to be done and how. This should include a description of the research design and any experimental manipulations.

Sample

If you are using human subjects you need to explain in this section who will participate in the study, how many participants there will be and how they will be selected.

Specifically, you should:
- define the survey or sample population
- specify the proposed sample size
- explain how the sample will be achieved – you should include details of selection and assignment procedures, payments made, location and types of institutions used (obviously the information to be included will depend on the project type)
- report the expected margins of error and design factors where appropriate.

Instruments

The research method (e.g. mail survey) or instrument (e.g. Stroop Colour-Word Test) used in the study needs to be described. You should also indicate why this is the best approach to take to gather your data.

The methodology of a qualitative research project is unlikely to be broken down into the sections outlined above. Rather, the researcher is more likely to be required to give a rationale for the use of the methodology and a brief description of the development of the method and its specific application in this study. Data collection methods should be detailed in full.

7.8 Ethical considerations

All research has ethical considerations and this section of your proposal may require considerable thought. Professional researchers are generally required by their professional bodies to abide by a code of practice. Most tertiary institutions have human ethics committees. Check to see whether you will need to consult this committee. A section of your proposal should outline the ethical considerations that will need to be addressed and identify the professional body that will oversee ethical practice. A detailed explanation of the ethical issues will not be required at the proposal stage but you should identify the key issues.

7.9 Budget

Although this section is not generally needed for undergraduate research, it is sensible to prepare a budget for any study requiring funds. For example, surveys typically incur costs for postage, stationery, telephone calls and computing, and sometimes for mailing lists, travel and accommodation. You need to be specific here. For example, if you are including in your budget a costing for transcribing interview tapes, it is not sufficient to give a lump sum for this cost. Instead you need to outline how many hours are required and the rate of pay per hour.

7.10 Timetable

This section should include an estimate of how long the project will take from the submission of the proposal, or the acceptance of the proposal, to the presentation of the final report, and specify expected completion dates for each stage of the research.

For projects that are undertaken in phases or require careful coordination with other events, a detailed timetable may be especially important. Task and date for each section of the work should be presented in two parallel columns.

7.11 References

All studies cited in the background section and the literature review should be properly referenced in this section, according to APA formatting conventions (see Chapter 12, page 89).

Finally

The formatting and content in this section refer to student proposals at undergraduate or postgraduate level. This chapter does not provide sufficient information for the purposes of applying for funding to outside funding agencies. You should refer to the guidelines provided by the funding agency for specific details of their requirements.

Research proposals checklist

1. Does my research proposal include all key sections?   Yes/No
2. Is my title page formatted correctly?   Yes/No
3. Has my background section established the relevance of the research?   Yes/No
4. Have I clearly stated the objectives?   Yes/No
5. Have I met the requirements of the literature review (see Ch. 8)?   Yes/No
6. Have I provided details of my proposal method and a rationale for its use?   Yes/No
7. Have I identified the key ethical issues?   Yes/No
8. Do my paragraphs have topic sentences?   Yes/No
9. Have I used clear language and effective sentence structure?   Yes/No
10. Have I used in-text references correctly?   Yes/No
11. Is my reference list formatted correctly?   Yes/No
12. Have I proofread my work?   Yes/No

8

LITERATURE REVIEWS

Students are unlikely to be asked to produce a literature review at 100 or 200 level. At more advanced levels, however, students may be asked to put together a literature review in the following contexts:
- as a stand-alone study
- as a preliminary section of a major research project.

A literature review is a summary of all the key research findings on a particular subject. It will teach you sophisticated library-search skills and the ability to organise material in a comprehensive manner.

A literature review should be extensive; students are expected to look beyond books and journal articles to all relevant sources: reports, government documents, review articles and newspapers may be relevant to some subject areas. The investigation is expected to be thorough; anticipate spending plenty of time in the library and do not hesitate to ask for advice from a librarian. An online search will also help.

8.1 The purpose of the literature review

There are five generally accepted purposes of the literature review. These are to:

1. Define and limit a problem

Most research areas are broad; a literature review identifies the key issues within a broad research area so that an area of interest that you might pursue can be defined.

2. Place your study in perspective

The purpose of academic research is to push out and add to the current body of knowledge within a particular field. Unless researchers are aware of the work of others, they cannot build upon an established foundation. A literature review allows the researcher to say:

'The work of A, B, and C has discovered this much about my question; the investigations of D have added this much to our knowledge. I propose to go beyond D's work in the following manner' (Ary, Jacobs & Razavieh, 1979, p. 57).

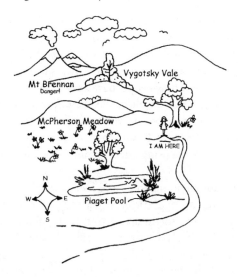

A literature review shows how your work is positioned in relation to the works of others.

3. Avoid unintentional replication of previous studies

Sometimes it is appropriate to replicate a previous study, but this should be done intentionally and for a particular purpose. A literature review helps you to make informed choices about a research topic within a scholarly context.

4. Select methods and measures

The success or failure of previous investigations can provide useful material when designing a research methodology. Students can assess what has worked before (or not worked) in previous contexts and why. Students may be alerted to new methodologies and procedures.

5. Relate findings to previous knowledge and suggest areas for further research

The findings of your research need to be related back to earlier studies. This 'places' your work and can point to areas that need further investigation.

8.2 Steps in writing a literature review

There are many approaches to writing a literature review. This is one approach that you might consider.

1. First of all, turn the topic into a question. For example, if you were writing a literature review about schools being sponsored by businesses, you might turn it into a question like this: 'Should schools be sponsored by businesses?'

2. Take your topic to the library and search for answers to this question. What you are looking for is an idea of how people have answered this question, the scope of the responses and related issues. Collect all your information. Search widely when you are reading for a literature review. You need to demonstrate that you are fully aware of the debate on the topic. Ensure that you have accessed all key writing in your field and that you are using quality sources (be especially careful with Internet sources).

3. Read through the material on the topic and see if you can divide it thematically. For example, if you were using the topic discussed above – 'Should schools be sponsored by business?' you might divide your material into two themes: 1. What are the critical issues? And 2. What are the various views? Once you've sorted out these main dividers, sort the material into piles. (Note: you might have more than two themes, or you might divide the material up chronologically.)

4. Take notes on all your material. If you do this on a computer, it will then be easy to divide up further. If you use pen and paper, number or label all your points (e.g. all the notes from researcher A should be labelled A) so that when you divide up the material, you know where it has come from. Focus on important material; don't get hung up on detailed results.

5. Now, focus on one theme/pile at a time. Read through your notes and see if you can see more sub-themes emerging from each theme. Sort your notes out into those sub-themes and write a heading for each one. See figure 8.1 for how this might be done with our example.

6. Taking your first theme (critical issues), write a summary or analysis of each sub-theme (e.g. ethical issues, competition – see figure 8.1). Don't worry about joining up the separate sub-themes, just write each one separately. What you need to focus on is 'what are the major ideas under this heading?' Try to deal with one idea per paragraph and start each paragraph with a summary of that idea (don't start off with 'X says …')

7. When you have written the sub-theme sections separately, write an introduction to that overall theme (e.g. critical issues).

8. Then write a conclusion for the section related to that theme overall.

9. Repeat steps 5–8 for each sub-theme.

10. Write a conclusion for the whole literature review. Remember, you don't have to come up with your own answer to the question (as you would in an essay, for example). But you do need to summarise an answer from the literature (e.g. 'While the literature on this topic seems very divided, certain key concerns stand out and it is clear that those most affected by sponsorship of schools are most opposed to this innovation.').

11. Write an introduction to the literature review that outlines why we should be interested in this question and what the major themes are.

12. Check that your headings are appropriate and write new ones if needed.

13. Edit your work; making sure that you answered your question clearly and that the main things come across clearly.

General objective: Should schools be sponsored by businesses?

1. What are the CRITICAL ISSUES concerning sponsorship of schools?
   1.1 Ethics
   1.2 Competition
   1.3 Misleading promotions
   1.4 Social equity issues

2. What are the VARIOUS VIEWS on sponsorship of schools?
   2.1 Principals' Association (–ve)
   2.2 Teachers (–ve)
   2.3 Government (+ve)
   2.4 Business leaders (+ve)
   2.5 Indigenous groups (+ve)

↓

→ danger of individual interference in curriculum (social? religious? agendas)
→ danger of reduced government funding
→ potential advantages to schools in high needs areas
→ our children are not a marketing opportunity

↓

→ views equally divided between –ve and +ve
→ those most involved are most opposed.
  – support for the proposal is largely related to economic issues
  – opposition to the proposal is largely associated with social equity and curriculum issues

Sponsorship of schools leads to questions of equity, integrity of curriculum and social agendas. Those most involved are critically concerned about these issues.

↓

Despite the advantages, the literature suggests no further sponsorship of schools without further investigation of the issues and careful (legislated?) safeguards.

Figure 8.1: Example of topic themes and sub-themes

A common mistake students make when writing literature reviews is that they just write a series of abstracts, so that each paragraph starts with 'Z says ... X says'. This is boring and not, ultimately, very useful. You need to organise the material you have found, as suggested here, so that the reader can see the main themes and issues raised by the question.

The literature review is sometimes asked for as a stand-alone assignment. But more commonly it is asked for as part of a research assignment. Its purpose is to position your research within an historical and theoretical framework. It defines the boundaries of a relevant scholarly debate and establishes your place within that debate. It looks back to past research to make sense of the present and point to the future.

Literature review checklist

1. Does my literature review address a clear question?   Yes/No
2. Do I explain in my introduction why this question is of interest?   Yes/No
3. Have I structured my literature review effectively?   Yes/No
4. Do my paragraphs have topic sentences?   Yes/No
5. Have I used in-text references correctly?   Yes/No
6. Have I avoided writing a series of abstracts?   Yes/No
7. Have I identified key themes in the literature?   Yes/No
8. Does my conclusion summarise the main ideas clearly?   Yes/No
9. Is my reference list formatted correctly?   Yes/No
10. Have I used quality sources?   Yes/No
11. Have I used clear sentences and eliminated clutter?   Yes/No
12. Have I proofread my work?   Yes/No

9

RESEARCH REPORTS

In education and in working towards a teaching qualification, you may be required to undertake small-scale research as part of your assignment requirements. The research approach that you take may involve working with quantitative data (data that can be measured and recorded in numbers) and/or qualitative data (data that is descriptive and recorded in words rather than numbers). Also the structure and style of a research report will vary considerably according to the research approach that you have used.

This chapter is designed as a basic introduction to writing research reports. If you are writing for post-graduate or other advanced courses or dealing with larger amounts of quantitative data, you will need to refer to the information in the Appendices of this manual, or to some of the titles on research writing listed in the Bibliography.

9.1 Style

The style of writing that you follow in your report will depend on your audience and on the type of research that you have undertaken. Often research reports are required to be written in quite a formal style. However, particularly when working with qualitative data, it may be appropriate to write using the first person (I or we). Always discuss with your lecturer whether a formal 'objective' style or a more informal style should be used for a particular project.

9.2 The structure of your research report

The structure of your research report will be set out in your assignment guidelines, but will generally follow a format that includes most or all of the following sections:
1. Title page
2. Acknowledgements
3. Contents
4. Abstract

5. Introduction
6. Literature review
7. Method
8. Results
9. Discussion
10. Conclusion
11. List of references
12. Appendices

This structure is a basic format for writing research reports, but particular lecturers may require you to adapt the format to suit a specific assignment. The following pages describe the basic content of each section of a research report. Use these pages as a guide for each section of your work.

In setting out your research report you should head each section and all subsections clearly.

The purpose of your report is to make clear to your audience:
- why you did your research (purpose)
- how you did your research (method)
- what you found out (results)
- what your findings mean (discussion and conclusions).

---

1. Title and title page

Your title should be short, specific and descriptive. It should clearly answer the question: 'What is this research about?' In other words, it should contain the key words of the report in a way that captures the interest of the reader.

The title page must contain the following information:
- the title of the report
- the name of the person or group by whom it is submitted
- the name of the person or group to whom it is submitted
- the date of submission
- course title and number

This information should be formatted as follows:

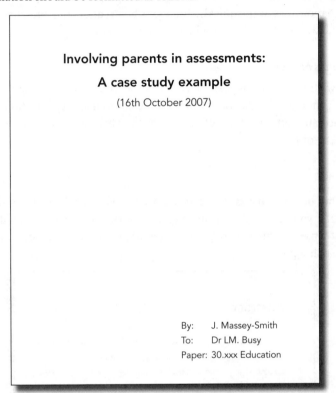

Involving parents in assessments:

A case study example

(16th October 2007)

By: J. Massey-Smith
To: Dr LM. Busy
Paper: 30.xxx Education

Figure 9.1: Format of a title page

2. Acknowledgements

You may wish to thank those who have participated or helped you in your research. (NB: Participants cannot be included if this will breach confidentiality, and you should ensure that you have their permission to include them in the Acknowledgements.) This section is optional.

3. Table of contents

In short research reports (under six pages) it may not be necessary to include a table of contents. The approach to setting out a table of contents is the same as the approach to writing a contents page for other reports (see page 33 for an example).

The table of contents is like an outline of the project, and helps the readers find the information they want quickly. It should be accurate and presented in a neat, professional way. Include page numbers and any appendices.

List of figures or tables

If you are writing a lengthy report at an advanced level, and are using many illustrations (e.g. tables, photographs, diagrams), they should be given in a separate list on a separate page immediately after the table of contents page. This page should be headed List of Tables or List of Figures.

4. Abstract

This may not be necessary. However, if you need to write an abstract it is always easier to do so after you have written your research report. Your abstract should be written in the past tense as a single paragraph. It should provide a very short clear summary of the research report.

Abstract

This study looks at the ways in which two primary schools responded to the interests and needs of children with disabilities through their language programs. The project adopted an action research approach, which involved the researcher as an active participant in considering and implementing change in each school. The research approach was collaborative and data was gathered from anecdotal records, document analysis, questionnaires and interviews. The project highlights the considerable difficulties faced in setting up language initiatives for children with disabilities and emphasises the need for considerable extra funding in this area.

Figure 9.2 Example of an abstract

The abstract should answer four key questions:
1. What is the purpose of the research?
2. How was the research carried out?
3. What were the main results?
4. What (if any) are the main conclusions?

5. Introduction

The Introduction should provide your reader with answers to the following questions:

1. Why did you do the research?
2. What was the purpose of the research?

This section should be short, so try to answer these questions as simply and clearly as possible. You are aiming to interest the reader in your topic and encourage them to read on, so lead them from information they already know to information they need to know.

The introduction should:
- explain any information that is necessary to put the research into context
- define the nature and scope of the focus of your research
- explain why you undertook the research – you should include relevant background information about the area that you are researching. This may involve summarising and referring to relevant literature. Keep this section brief if you are required to write a literature review as part of your research report. If you are not including a literature review, you may need to make this section longer
- Give details of specific objectives or research questions that will be considered in your research.

Introduction

Bandura first proposed his theory of self-efficacy in 1977, and since that time it has created a great deal of research interest. Bandura (1977) postulates that self-efficacy expectations, that is, a person's beliefs concerning his or her ability to successfully perform a given task or behaviour, are a major determinant of whether that individual will perform the task

In the domain of education, one line of study researchers are interested in is the relationship between mathematics self-efficacy and mathematics performance...

The purpose of the present study was to explore the self-efficacy/performance relationship in the area of mathematics achievement. The research question for the study is as follows:

'Is Self-efficacy with regard to specific mathematics problems related to actual performance on an equivalent set of problems?'

Figure 9.3: Example of part of an introduction

6. Literature review

Writing a literature review is covered in Chapter 8 of this book.

7. Research design/method

This section answers the questions:

1. How did you conduct your research?
2. Why did you do it that way?

In this section of your report you need to provide precise details on how the research was conducted. In some types of research, it is important that the research is able to be repeated. Your description of the research method you have used should contain enough detail to provide a 'recipe' that another researcher could follow if they wished to repeat your study.

In order to make sure that this section of your report is clearly structured, you may find it helpful to use the following sub-sections.

(a) Participants

Describe the participants in the research. If, for example, you are undertaking research in a classroom or early childhood setting, this would include information about the number of children included in your research, the ages of the children and other information relevant to your research focus.

If you are not including all the members of a particular group (e.g. class/school) then you should describe how and why you selected the sample for research.

Participants

All the subjects (172 women; 124 men) were students enrolled in an introductory psychology course at a university in New Zealand. It is unlikely that this sample is representative of all introductory psychology students in New Zealand. Subjects ranged in age from 17 to 66 years, with a mean age of 27 (SD = 22 years). Almost all the subjects were of European descent (83%).

Figure 9.4: Example of a participants sub-section

(b) Context

Include relevant details about the context in which you are undertaking your research. For example, it may be important to provide information about the institution or community in which you are undertaking your research.

(c) Ethical considerations

Explain any ethical considerations and steps taken to protect confidentiality and privacy. If you have used a popular code of ethics or had approval from an institution's ethics committee, you should state this.

(d) Instruments and materials

Describe any instruments or materials used, including videos, tape recorders, checklists, questionnaires, tests and so on. If you are using standard tests or procedures you do not need to describe these in detail; however, if you are using data gathering techniques such as questionnaires or interviews that you have devised yourself, you will need to provide more detail. It is often useful to provide copies of any such material as an appendix to your report.

Instruments and materials

Mathematics self-efficacy scale:

The mathematics self-efficacy scale contains 35 items tapping into mathematics-related self-efficacy expectation. The scale is composed of two subscales: (a) the Mathematics Tasks subscale, consisting of 18 items involving everyday tasks such as balancing a chequebook etc, and (b) the Mathematics Problems subscale, consisting of 17 arithmetic, algebraic and geometric problems.

Students were asked to rate their confidence in their ability to successfully (a) perform the task and (b) solve the problems. Confidence ratings for both cases were made on a 7 point continuum from 'no confidence at all' (0) to 'complete confidence' (6).

Both the total scale and the subscales have high internal consistency and high re-test reliabilities, and report to be valid.

Figure 9.5: Example of an instruments and materials section

(e) Procedure

This is the 'how' section of the report. It should be written in the past tense and you should present your points in a logical order. Describe events in the order that they took place.

Each step of your procedure needs to be described clearly and concisely. It may also be important to explain why you chose to undertake specific steps in the research.

Procedure

Information about the study was provided to all subjects. For example, all subjects were informed of their rights to withdraw from the study at any time or refuse to answer any particular question. The mathematics self-efficacy and mathematics performance instruments were administered to all subjects at the same point in time, in place of a scheduled lecture. This ensured that subjects received exactly the same instructions and also that there was no passing on of information between groups.

Figure 9.6: Example of a procedure section

(f) Limitations

If there are any limitations to the method you have used (and there usually are!) say what they are clearly.

8. Results

The results section answers the question:

What did you find or see?

In very short reports, you may decide to combine your Results and Discussion sections. However, in most instances, it is clearer to include a separate section that summarises your results before you go on to your Discussion.

In writing up your results you need to include only the information that is relevant to the purposes of your research as set out in the Introduction. In almost any research project you are likely to find out about many more things than are included in the actual focus of your research, but if they are not relevant to your focus then they should be left out.

You should present your results in a logical sequence. For example, it may be helpful to follow the order of the research objectives or research question identified in your introduction. Alternatively you may find that following the sequence identified in the Procedure section of your methods is an appropriate way to structure this section of your report.

Use sub-headings if they make it easier for your reader to see your results.

Make sure that any figures, tables, graphs or other visual information is labelled and titled clearly. Always explain the significance of this material in words. However, avoid lengthy descriptions of information that is clear to the reader from looking at figures or tables. Perhaps emphasise the main points (briefly) but do not put the graph or table into words and hence present your results twice. (Note: If it is clearer to give the information in words rather than using a table or graph, do not use a table or graph!)

• *Qualitative data*

Results drawn from qualitative data are likely to be presented in text, though it may also be appropriate to supplement your text with visual material or samples of evidence (e.g. examples of children's work).

In working with qualitative data, you should summarise your results succinctly and clearly. It will not be possible to include everything that you found. It may be appropriate to include more detailed information, such as transcripts of interview material or classroom interactions, diary excerpts or questionnaire responses in your appendices. You may also find in summarising data obtained in these ways that it is useful to quote from your data.

• ***Quantitative data***
Quantitative data can often be presented very briefly by summarising data using tables, charts or graphs. A full description of how to present quantitative data is provided in Appendix E, page 127.

Results

In order to ascertain the relationship between mathematics self-efficacy and mathematics performance, correlation analyses were performed. The overall correlation coefficient between self-efficacy and performance was .48, indicating a moderately strong positive relationship. This correlation only provides partial support for the study hypothesis, since, although it is in the anticipated direction, it is not as large as expected. The coefficients for the self-efficacy subscales (Tasks subscale and Problems subscale) and performance were .38 and .41 respectively. All correlations were significant at the .01 level.

Figure 9.9: Example of part of a results section

9. Discussion

This section of the report should explain the significance of your results.

It can be useful to begin the discussion by restating the original research question objectives or question.

The following are features of a good discussion:
• First, discuss. Do not restate the results. Instead, try to present the principles and relationships shown by the results.
• Link your results and findings to the literature on the topic (as outlined in the literature review).
• Point out any exceptions or unexpected results. Do not try to 'fudge' or cover up data that does not quite fit.
• Discuss what your results mean in relation to the initial research question or objectives.
• Consider the relevance, usefulness and limitations of your study. Be honest. If you recognise a problem/limitation, say so.
• Be careful that you do not get carried away with sweeping generalisations or unsubstantiated speculation.

The main parts of the discussion should be presented in order of importance – or in the same order as the main points in the results section and objectives (ideally, both alternatives should come together). Do not be tempted to start with insignificant points and build up to your main point; state the main points early, and each main point at the beginning of a paragraph, so that the reader can easily locate the key points made.

Show how your findings relate to other work in the field (i.e. make connections with your literature review).

- If your findings replicate what has been found by other researchers, then you should point this out.
- If your findings are not consistent with other research, you will need to discuss this and provide suggestions or explanations for this.
- If your research provides new insights and adds to the body of knowledge on the subject, then state or show what is new in your work and why your results are important (do not make your claims too extravagant though!).

Discussion

The findings lend support to Bandura's (1977) assertion that self-efficacy is a moderate to strong predictor of behaviour, and the current study demonstrates this in the domain of mathematics performance. However, the correlations between mathematics self-efficacy and performance were lower than expected.

Future research might include more generalised measures of mathematical performance. This should permit a replication of the present study findings, and also produce stronger correlations between mathematics self-efficacy and mathematics problems.

Figure 9.10: Example of part of a discussion section

10. Conclusion

The conclusion should 'wrap up' the report by summarising the major points made in the discussion in relation to your objectives or research question. It should be kept short and to the point. Avoid banal statements such as 'this study has pointed to some interesting implications for research in the field'. Statements like this add nothing of use or interest to the reader. Discuss any limitations of the study.

It may be relevant for some studies to end with a list or short discussion of specific recommendations for directions of further research.

11. References

Every report that draws on other people's ideas or findings must have a reference section where the sources are cited in full.

The reference section lists all the sources that have been cited in the report. In other words, if you have sources but have not cited them, they should not appear in your references. If you have sources that have been influential but not cited, they should be listed under the heading Bibliography, and should immediately follow your list of references.

Format your reference list and bibliography according to APA conventions (see Chapter 12, page 89).

12. Appendices

Material that is complex and/or detailed is collected at the end of the report in the appendices section so as not to distract readers from the main theme.

Appendices can contain supplementary illustrative material that a reader may want to refer to after they have read the report (for example, questionnaires, letters, pamphlets, all of which illustrate some aspects of the material discussed in the text).

Appendices are also useful a useful place to include detailed explanations of a model or procedure referred to in the discussion. If some specialist readers – but not most readers – would want certain material, it should be placed in an appendix.

Appendices should always be presented in a professional manner, so do not be tempted just to fold up all your computer print-out figures and staple them to the end of your report! You still need to organise and select material and present it in a way that is easily understood by your reader.

Appendices should always be given a number or letter and title. For example,

Appendix A: Key findings regarding birth order

or

Appendix 1: International Comparison of Early Childhood Participation Rates

When referring to an appendix in the body of a report, explain its significance. Do not just add 'refer to appendices 1, 3 and 7' to the end of a sentence. Rather, explain to the reader how the appendix will be of use to them. For example, 'Refer to Appendix A for a more detailed description of this model'.

Appendices should:

- provide a detailed explanation serving the needs of some specialised readers
- be clearly and neatly set out
- be numbered (or lettered)
- be given a title
- be arranged in the order that they are mentioned in the text
- be related to the report's objectives and not just 'tacked on'.

10

POLICY DOCUMENTS/POLICY WRITING

Within educational studies you may be required to prepare policy documents. This is something that you are likely to be involved with at some stage if you are working in an educational institution. This chapter provides guidelines for writing policy documents. The policy you write may be the result of a 'policy brief' or report in which you have analysed and researched a specific situation (see for example 'reports to a client') While the core policy document that you prepare may be very brief, you are also likely to be required to provide:

- an implementation plan that provides detailed information on who will be involved with the implementation of policy, the steps that must be taken to ensure that policy is implemented, how the policy will be made known to all involved, training and expenses that may be needed and so on
- policy background and rationale that provides general background to the policy and the problem or issue that the policy addresses. The rationale also explains or discusses the purpose of the policy and the reasons that guidelines set out in the policy document have been identified

> **CAUTION**
>
> Although most policies follow a similar pattern, your lecturer or tutor may provide you with a specific format that differs from the guidelines provided in this chapter. You should adapt the following information to fit the specific requirements of the assignment or institution for which you are writing policy.

10.1 What is policy?

The purpose of a policy is to provide a guide for decision-making and action. Policies are usually developed in response to a problem, need or issue of some importance. They are needed in situations where there may be differing perspectives and interests or in which there is uncertainty, vagueness or confusion.

Policies should reflect a set of beliefs, values or philosophy on the issues. Not all issues need policies – routine matters can usually be managed with a document that sets out procedures. So, for example, it may be appropriate to have a policy on behaviour or homework, but a procedural document may be all that is needed to deal with collection of lunch orders.

Most policies consist of a statement of purpose and one or more broad guidelines as to how that purpose is to be achieved. In general, policies:

- have institution-wide application
- provide a framework or guidelines that either constrain or mandate action
- are broad enough for those involved to exercise some discretion in meeting day-to-day situations that arise. The policy needs to be able to 'fit' a variety of contexts within the institution
- set guidelines for the foreseeable future and will change infrequently
- are brief (ideally, policies should generally be less than one page in length).

> The most important rule to keep in mind when writing any policy is to ensure that it is written in clear, concise and simple language.

Policies are generally written for diverse audiences, so it is usually important that they are jargon-free. The audience for educational policy is likely to include not only professionals but also parents and/or students. Sometimes, policies can be adapted for two different audiences e.g. children and adults.

Visual aids can be very useful in presenting information clearly in policy documents, so you should consider using charts or tables if appropriate. Tables, flow charts and other visual aids should be numbered consecutively in your policy document.

Effective policies ensure that there is consistency in decisions and actions within the institution. They provide a clear basis for rules and procedures. Good policies clarify obligations and responsibilities: they let individuals know what is expected of them and they also make it clear why certain actions are required. They provide positive direction for members of the institution, even though they do not necessarily specify the methods that should be used to achieve the desired results. In effect, good policy provides guidance but also provides room for individuals or groups to make professional judgements. Good policy ensures that the rights and well-being of individuals and groups within the educational community are respected, and that the goals and aims of the institution are furthered.

10.2 Policy development

In developing policy you need to:
1. Identify the problem, issue or need. What is happening now? What needs to change?
2. Collect relevant background information and material. This will include;
    - relevant institutional documents such as existing policies, mission statements, statements of philosophy and so on
    - relevant state or national policies, curriculum statements and so on if appropriate
    - relevant information in the literature
    - relevant opinions of those involved (note: in general, policies require considerable consultation with those who will be affected by the policy. However, this may not be possible if the policy you are developing is 'hypothetical' and for assignment purposes only.)
3. Identify key ideas:
    - Why do you want the policy?
    - What are the key beliefs or philosophy of the institution in relation to the issue?
    - What exactly do you want the policy to say?
    - What actions do you want to happen as a result of the policy?
4. Draft your policy statement based on background information and key ideas. Sometimes it can be helpful to apply your policy to hypothetical situations, or examples that have occurred in the past to 'test' the policy. If you followed the policy, would it effectively provide a basis or guide for action that would be considered desirable?

10.3 Policy format

Your policy may include the following sections, depending on the length and purpose required:

Table of Contents	If your policy document as a whole is lengthy, and includes detailed background information and appendices for example, it may be useful to include a detailed table of contents that lists major headings and sub-headings as well as page number references.
Policy	This section should be brief and clear (no more than one page if possible). It may include: • statement of purpose (rationale/goal) • guidelines • definitions (this should only include those terms essential to the reader's understanding of the basic policy)
Implementation plan	As discussed below, this information may be most clearly presented in table or diagrammatic form, so that times, tasks and responsibilities are easily identified.
Policy background and rationale	For assignment purposes, this is likely to be the section of your policy as a whole in which you provide evidence of your understanding of relevant literature in helping you analyse the situation and make decisions about policy. To some extent this section of your policy may form the 'body' of your assignment and you may need to provide more explanation and follow a more academic style of presentation than would otherwise be required.
Reference List	A list of all information that you have referred to, presented in APA format.
Related information	This should list any related information that is mentioned in the policy and information plan (e.g. other policies, documents, legislation).
Contact people	This list should include contact information on how to contact key people who are able to answer questions or provide further information.
Appendices	This section should contain any further relevant documentation or information.

10.4 Policy section

Statement of purpose

This should be a brief statement that clearly and simply identifies the philosophy that underpins the policy as well as the overall purpose of the policy. This should arise from the broader goals of the institution.

Statement of purpose

'Selwyn College is committed to ensuring that all staff and students are able to work and learn in an environment free from harassment.' (Office of the Race Relations Conciliator, page 40)

Figure 10.1: Example of a statement of purpose section

In some policies the statement of purpose is divided into two sections that identify the rationale (or philosophy) and goal separately. Note: in the example below a clear definition of 'racial harassment' is included within the rationale.

Rationale

Racial harassment refers to racially based, unwelcome behaviour that any person on Hagley Community College site may find personally offensive, may affect morale, and may interfere with the teaching and learning processes or the work effectiveness within the College environment.

Goal

To create and maintain a safe multicultural environment at Hagley Community college where racial harassment is neither tolerated nor condoned.

(Office of the Race Relations Conciliator, p.48)

Figure 10.2: Example of a divided statement of purpose

Guidelines

Guidelines should clearly set out what is required of participants. In developing guidelines you should keep in mind the following points:

1. Select your words carefully.

   For example, words like 'should' may imply a choice where choice is not intended. *'Teachers should not smoke within school premises'* implies that while it's preferable that teachers not smoke, it is ok if they do. It is much clearer to say that, *'Teachers must not smoke within school premises'.*

2. Use as few words as possible.

   For example, words like 'all' can be redundant. *'All children will be assigned homework on a regular basis.'* Children/teachers/staff and so on will naturally imply 'all' unless it is stated otherwise.

10.5 Implementation plan

This section of policy is crucial in ensuring that policy is actually translated successfully into action. Key questions that should be considered in establishing your implementation plan are likely to include some, if not all, of the following:

- What is the approval process for the policy? Does the policy require approval from relevant management, statutory or community groups?
- Who should know this policy? Who are the groups or individuals who are affected by the policy (students, teachers, parents, administrators, management and so on)?
- How will the policy be disseminated? How will those affected by the policy be contacted? How will the policy be displayed?
- Who is going to be responsible for implementing and acting on aspects of the policy? What are the specific roles, responsibilities and actions required by policy? What are the lines of accountability in implementing policy?
- What training or staff development will be needed in order to implement policy effectively?
- What is the timeline or sequence for implementation? (Relevant dates for specific actions should be identified.)
- What are the procedures for complaint, query or non-compliance? Who are the key contact people that those involved with policy can go to for advice?
- What are the procedures for evaluation and review of the policy? Does the policy have an 'expiry date'? Is there a set date for review?

There may be a set format for setting out an implementation plan within your institution or within your assignment guidelines. If this is not the case, as with other aspects of your policy, your format is likely to be guided by the intention to make the information as clear and unambiguous as possible to your intended audience. It is often useful to present implementation information in table or flow chart format.

10.6 Policy background and rationale: Why are we doing it?

The actual policy should not explain or justify itself, even though this may be evident in the statement of purpose. In general when a policy is being proposed or presented to others, it is important to provide an account of *why* the policy was developed. It is also usually necessary to provide some explanation of why specific guidelines have been chosen.

Your rationale will probably include:
- clarification and discussion of any terms that are used within the policy and are essential to the reader's understanding of the policy
- legal or regulatory requirements
- a description of the original issue, problem or need, as well as any relevant information about what has happened in the past
- relevant information from other sources (especially from relevant research and discussion in the literature)
- acknowledgement of the interests of all those affected
- overall benefits.

The key ideas and background information that you have collected in developing your policy (see 10.2 above) will provide the basis for your rationale.

For assignment purposes, it is likely to be important that you provide considerable reference to material from relevant literature within your rationale. In this instance it is appropriate that your rationale is presented in standard academic style, and APA format should be followed in citing and quoting within this section of the assignment.

However, if you are presenting your policy to members of the educational community (e.g. children or parents) it may be more appropriate to provide a rationale that avoids jargon and a more academic style. For some audiences, it may be appropriate to include a list of references or resources for further information within appendices that may be attached to the policy document.

You may find that information in your rationale is presented most clearly if you use separate headings for each section.

10.7 Appendices

Your appendices should contain any further information that may be of use to those who will be using or reading your policy. This section of a policy generally includes any information that would make other sections of the policy unnecessarily long or inaccessible.

For example, your appendices may contain:

- an overall flow chart of policy implementation (especially if this has not been included in the earlier section of your policy)
- a detailed flow chart of relevant processes
- diagrammatic details of lines of authority/responsibility
- a glossary of definitions or explanations of relevant terminology (but remember key terms that are essential to a reader's understanding of policy should be included within the policy document or rationale)
- copies of specific legal or regulatory documents that are particularly relevant to the policy
- details of references and resource materials that may be relevant to specific groups involved in policy implementation.

10.8 Checklist

Key questions: Have you followed the format advised in your assignment guidelines?

Is the language that you have used clear and appropriate to the intended audience for this policy?

Table of Contents	Have you set out headings, sub-headings and page numbers clearly?
Policy	Are essential terms clearly explained?
	Have you used words which are clear and direct?
	Have you cut out any extra words that are not needed?
	Is the policy less than one page in length?
Implementation plan	Is the information set out clearly?
	Is it easy to see who is responsible for what actions?
	Are time requirements identified clearly?

Policy background and rationale	Does this section discuss the questions? Why do we need a policy (background/problem/legal requirements)? What is the purpose of the policy (how does this further philosophy of the institution)? Why have specific guidelines been chosen? What will be the benefit of the policy? Have you defined terms which have special meanings? If you have used someone else's ideas or information have you cited their name and date of publication?
Reference List	If you have cited research, information or ideas in your policy, is the source listed in your reference list? Is your reference list in alphabetic order? Have you used APA format?
Related information	Have you included a list of relevant, policies, or legislation?
Contact people	Have you included a list of key contacts with relevant detalis?
Appendices	Are your appendices clearly numbered, labelled and referenced?

11

EDITORIAL STYLE

The presentation of an assignment is important. A well-prepared document looks professional and credible. Clear presentation can prevent misinterpretation of content and helps the reader understand the material.

The following guidelines should be considered suggestions for effective presentation rather than directives. Be flexible and consider the needs of the reader and the format of a particular assignment when deciding on appropriate presentation.

11.1 Page numbering

Each page of an assignment (except the title page) should be numbered, with the number centred at the bottom of the page. Pages preceding the body of a report (e.g. Executive Summary, Table of Contents) are numbered in Roman numerals. In the body of all assignments, the pages are numbered in Arabic numerals.

11.2 Line spacing

Most assignments should be double spaced so that there is room for the marker's comments.

For reports, each major section should begin on a new page.

11.3 Headings and numbering

Where headings are appropriate, major section headings should be capitalised and, where appropriate, numbered 1, 2, 3, etc. Sub-headings within each section should be capitalised lowercase, and numbered 1.1, 1.2, etc. An assignment should require no more than two levels of numbered headings (1.4.3.7 is difficult for the reader to understand within the context of the structure of your work). If you find that you do need sub-sections, do not number the minor headings.

All headings should be printed in bold and begin at the left margin. Headings at the top level should be in capitals; only the first letter of each major word should be capitalised for headings at lower levels. Only use one kind of font: a range of font styles looks messy.

```
1. INTRODUCTION
       1.1    Background of the Company
              History
              Management
              Structure

2. DISCUSSION
       2.2    Breakdown of Authority
              Senior Management
              Supervisors



                      2
```

Figure 11.1: Levels and Presentation of Headings

Remember, the presentation of your work is important to aid the reader's understanding and to help establish your own professionalism.

11.4 Paragraphs

You may choose one of two approaches to setting and paragraphs. Either the text should be flush with the left margin and left-justified, or you may indent the first line of each paragraph and omit the blank space between paragraphs.

Paragraphs should begin two blank lines under top level or second-level headings, and one line under lower-level headings. Leave a single blank line between paragraphs.

11.5 Quotations in the text

See Appendix A, Using material from written sources, page 101.

11.6 Acronyms

Acronyms are used to abbreviate long titles or clumsy expressions. Examples include NZ for New Zealand and CEO for Chief Executive Officer.

Acronyms are acceptable as long as they do not detract from the reader's easy understanding of the text. If too many unfamiliar acronyms are used the reader may need to continually check meanings, which may affect their understanding of and response to your text. For this reason, use acronyms cautiously.

The first time an acronym is presented it should be written out in full and the acronym should be placed in brackets immediately afterwards (e.g. Ted's Personal Assistant (PA) acted as gatekeeper in this situation).

From then on the acronym can be used without further explanation.

Print acronyms without spaces or stops, for example:

USA	not	U S A	or	U.S.A.
SUWAC	not	S U W A C	or	S.U.W.A.C

11.7 Numbers

The general rule is to use words to express numbers below 10 and numerals to express numbers 10 and above. However, numbers coming at the beginning of a sentence should be expressed as words, for example:

> Twelve officers remained on the scene and four of these were to remain there throughout the night. The next day, reinforcements of 24 men were brought in, 12 of whom combed the adjacent area.

11.8 Inclusive language

Language presents our view of the world. If you write 'every principal must develop the trust and confidence of his staff', you are saying that you think all principals are male (which they are not) or that those principals who are not male do not mind being thought of as male – which is definitely not a safe assumption!

- don't use 'man' to apply to men and women – rephrase inclusively
- use 'they' or 'he/she' rather than 'he' to denote the third person
- do not assume that people in certain occupation or positions are a particular gender
- do not use 'girl' to refer to a grown woman, *in any context!*

11.9

Your style for all assignments should be formal but clear. Avoid casual expressions. Imagine you are a professional writing to another professional whose opinions you respect.

12

REFERENCING—APA STYLE

Referencing is an important part of all academic work. Sources of information should be acknowledged for the following reasons:
- to distinguish between your ideas and someone else's.
- to show readers the range and quality of your reading.
- to direct readers to the sources used, if they want further information.

Failure to acknowledge a source of information, or using other people's ideas as your own, is called *plagiarism*, and is a serious form of academic dishonesty.

While there are many different sets of conventions for referencing – and if you ever publish research you will find that many journals have their own in-house style – many social science courses use the formatting conventions of the American Psychological Association for setting out references. Some of these conventions are listed below. For more detail on APA referencing you should refer to the *Publication Manual of the American Psychological Association* (5th ed.).

12.1   Acknowledging sources

The APA style of referencing uses in-line acknowledgement of sources rather than footnotes or endnotes. This means that sources need to be acknowledged in the ways listed below.

1. How do I acknowledge an idea which I have expressed in my own words?

Sometimes someone else's ideas, concepts or figures, but not that person's exact words may be included in your work. This is called citing or paraphrasing (as opposed to quoting, when you use someone's exact words). In this situation, the source must be acknowledged by putting the author's last name and the date when the work was published in brackets at the end of the sentence.

> Management consultants usually see the formulation of a strategic plan as an essential step for all organisations (McKendrey, 2002).
>
> Many entrepreneurs see educational qualifications as irrelevant (Fergusson, 2001; McKendrey, 2002).

Note that in the second example above, where two sources are cited, each one is separated with a semicolon.

Another approach to this is to include the surname of the author within your sentence with the date in brackets, like this:

> As McKendrey (2002) suggests, entrepreneurs see educational qualifications as irrelevant.

2. How do I include a short quotation in my work?

If the author's own words are being used, put the quotation in quotation marks and include a page number at the end of the reference.

> For many Australians, this country is no longer an agricultural nation. Australia has grown, diversified and bounced back again, determined never again to be reliant on a single industry and market. 'We have come of age, internationally' (Anderson, 2002, p.64).

NB: When the quotation ends a sentence, the full stop comes *after* the information in brackets.

3. How do I include a longer quotation in my work?

If a direct quotation which is longer than either two sentences or 20 words is being used, the quotation should be indented five spaces and quotation marks *omitted*. The reference should be acknowledged in the same way as the shorter quotation above.

> Within management theory there have been many changes and developments. One researcher – Sharryn Williams – has identified a key factor for management sources: communication.
>
> > Communication is a vital factor in determining managerial success. A successful manager establishes links throughout her organisation, formal and informal, upwards, downwards and horizontally. Two vital measures of success are these:

> a respect for formal procedures and a recognition of the value of the informal network (2003, p.6).
>
> Such a perspective has support from many other theorists in the area…

4. How do I reference an author who is quoted in a book/journal I am reading?

If you wish to use a quotation or cite an idea which is quoted or cited by another author, then both sources should be acknowledged in the text as follows:

> Although much has been written about the negative impact of stress, 'nevertheless, stress can contribute to performance' (Ward, 1998, p.33 cited in Bowling, 2001, p.16).
>
> Although many authors have emphasised the way in which stress can impact negatively on performance, Ward (1998, cited in Bowling, 2001) emphasises its positive aspects.

The Reference list, at the end of the assignment, would list only Bowling, *not* Ward.

5. How do I reference a source if I have already used the author's name in the sentence?

Sometimes an author may be directly referred to within the assignment.

> - Magnall (1994) was the first to maintain that …
> - Planning is the first essential step according to Magnall (1994).
> - Researchers in the field (Magnall, 1994; Crews, 2002) indicate that …
> - He stated that 'the management cycle has four key elements' (Magnall, 1994, p.16) but did not rank those four factors.

6. How do I reference two works by the same author?

If referring to two or more works by the same author, both published in the same year, the first has an 'a' after the date, the second has a 'b' and so on:

> In her next study of the problem (Lenart, 2001b), she considered other factors.

The author's name would then appear twice (or more often) in the references section at the end of the paper, with the appropriate small letter beside the date.

7. How do I reference a work with many authors?

If a work has three or more authors, all names should be listed in the first citation, but et al. (meaning 'and others') may be used in subsequent citations:

First citation	Coles, Emerson & Ormsby (1992) found that ...
Subsequent citations	Coles et al. (1992) also found ...

8. How do I reference a letter, email or interview?

Anything that isn't accessible to other people (i.e. not published in any way) is called a personal communication. It is not included in the reference list but should be cited in the text. Give initials of the communicator and an exact date.

> (E. C. MacKay, personal communication, 9 December 2001)

9. How do I reference something with no author, such as some newspaper articles or legal material?

If you are referring to something that has no acknowledged author, then substitute the first few words of the title in single quotation marks.

> ('Dollar plummets', 2004)

Most legal material is cited in text in this way, but details of how specific types of legal material should be formatted in the text may be found in appendix D of the *APA Style Manual* (5th ed.) or visit http://www.lib.wsc.ma.edu/legalapa.htm.

10. How do I cite an electronic source (e.g. a web page) in the body of an argument?

A web page or website is acknowledged in the text in the same way as other texts, i.e. you state the author (or corporate author), year of publication, and a page number for a direct quote. If no page numbers are indicated in the source, give paragraph number e.g. (McKenzie, 2004, para 14).

More ephemeral forms of electronic sources, e.g. email, forum discussion etc., should be referenced as personal communications.

12.2   What is a reference list?

A reference list is a list of the full bibliographical details of all the material quoted or cited in your assignment. Every assignment written must have a reference list. It should be started on a new page and be headed 'References'.

In listing the references at the end of the document, one style guide should be followed consistently. We recommend that you use the following format, taken from the *Publication Manual of the American Psychological Association (APA)* (5th ed.).[1]

All items must be listed in alphabetical order, according to the surname of the first author.

1. How do I list a book according to APA style?

Put the author's surname first, spelt out in full, with initials only for first and second names. Give the date of publication in brackets. Next comes the *title*, city of publication and publisher. Note that on the reference page only the first letter of the first word of the title and subtitle is capitalised. Title and subtitle should be underlined or italicised. Either is acceptable. The title is followed by a full stop. A colon (:) separates the place of publication from the publisher's name.

The following list gives examples of the most commonly used types of referencing using this referencing style.

a. *Single author*

>   Sligo, F. (1991). *Organisational behaviour: Case studies and commentaries.* Palmerston North: Dunmore Press.

b. *Single author, later edition*

>   May, C. (1992). *Effective writing: A handbook for accountants* (3rd ed.). Englewood Cliffs, New Jersey: Prentice-Hall, Inc.

c. *Two authors*

>   Strunk, W. Jr, & White, E.B. (1979). *The elements of style* (3rd ed.). New York: Macmillan.

d. *Corporate author*

>   American Psychological Association. (2004). *Publication manual of the American Psychological Association* (5th ed.). Washington, DC: Author.

e. Edited book

> Jackson, R., & Buckland, T. (eds). (1992). *Summer schools: A unique grouping.* London: Oxford University Press.

f. Article or chapter in edited book

> Mellallieu, P.J. (1993). The postmodernist manager. In P.J. Mellallieu and N. Boneparte (Eds), *The manager: Missionary, magician and megalomaniac* (pp.134–59). New York: John Wiley and Sons.

2. How do I reference a periodical?

Periodicals are anything that is published on a regular basis – magazines, journals and newspapers. Sometimes it is difficult to distinguish between journals and magazines, but here is a general rule of thumb: if the articles in the periodical have a reference section (i.e. if they list their sources in some academically conventional way) then it can be regarded as a journal; if they do not have a reference section, then treat it as a magazine.

Periodicals are referenced as follows:

Titles of periodicals should be quoted in full and italicised and followed by volume numbers, italicised, and page numbers, not italicised. Titles of articles should not be italicised, underlined or placed in inverted commas.

a. Journal article, one author

> Ferguson, I.S. (2003). Forecasting the future for timber. *The Australian Journal of Agricultural Economics, 18,* 562–78.

b. Journal article, two authors, journal paginated by issue

> Becker, L.J., & Seligman, C. (2001). Welcome to the energy crisis. *Journal of Social Issues, 37,* 2, 1–7.

Note that: if the journal is paginated by volume rather than issue, then you do not include the issue number.

c. Magazine article

> Emerson, A.M. (2004, 10–17 December). Bald is beautiful. *The Listener,* 16.

d. Newspaper article, no author

> Students attack Todd report. (2004, 16 June). *The Dominion,* 3.

e. Newspaper article, author known

Robinson, L. (2004, 19 July). The new orthodoxy. *The Dominion*, 9.

f. Newsletter article, corporate author

Staff (2002, 3 September). Why students should pay more. *National Business Review*, 7.

3. How do I reference Internet sources?

a. Webpage

O'Connor, R.E. (2004). *Managing music*. Retrieved 19 August, 2004 from http://www.musicresourcesNZ/management.asp.

b. Online periodical

Hills, S.J. (2003). Soaring above: Managing educational change. *Education Resource Management in Aotearoa/New Zealand, 16*, 443-449. Retrieved 24 March, 2003 from http://www.EdResource.massey.ac.nz/management/focus.asp.

Note re author: if the web page does not have a specified author, see if you can find a corporate author. If neither is available, move the title into the author's position.

Note re access details: always provide the full URL and the exact date of retrieval. Since materials on the Internet can change very quickly, you must be exact about the timing and location of your source material.

Note re date: if no date is available, put n.d. in the date position.

4. How do I reference technical research reports?

Hewitt, A. (1999). *Sexual stereotyping in advertisements for children* (Report No. 634–3964). Washington DC: International Marketing Association.

5. How do I reference unpublished theses?

Knowles, G.A. (2001). New methods for old. Unpublished doctoral dissertation, Massey University, Palmerston North, New Zealand.

Frawley, E.A. (2002). Nobody does it better; English sheep farmers face the world. Unpublished master's thesis, Sussex University, Brighton.

6. How do I reference annual reports?

Annual reports are referenced as books with corporate authors (see above).

7. How do I reference study guide material?

If you cite articles or excerpts from books which are reprinted in Study Guides, refer to the article or book directly (your Study Guide *should* contain full bibliographical information!)

   If the material being cited is not part of a reprinted article or book, it should be referenced as follows:

a. *Where the study guide has an identified author:*

> Emerson, J.M. (2004). *Teaching the gifted child: Study guide 2.* Palmerston North: College of Education, Massey University.

b. *Where the study guide has no identified author:*

> Department of Management Systems, College of Business. (2004). *26.120 Introduction to organisation and management.* Palmerston North: Massey University.

8. How do I reference abstracts from a database or from a list of abstracts?

> James, F., & Burrow, G.M. (2002). The pessimistic manager meets the marketing manager. *Journal of Multi-Strategic Development, 19,* 417–20. Abstract retrieved 19 November, 2004, from ERIC database.

9. How do I cite computer programs?

> Picard, J.L. (1995). Captain's log: Metacognitive modelling (Version 5.0) [Computer Software]. Paris: Enterprise Software Services, Inc.

10. How do I cite a personal communication?

Sometimes you will need to acknowledge personal communication as a source of information. This includes lecture notes, memos, e-mail messages, interviews and the like. Personal communication is NOT included in a reference list or bibliography – you should only cite personal communications in the text of your assignment.

11. Where do I find information about referencing materials not mentioned here?

For details on how to format other, more unusual material (e.g. proceedings of meetings and symposia, films, TV programs, individual interviews) refer to the *Publication Manual of the American Psychological Association*, Edition 5, also referred to as the APA Style Manual. Another useful source of information is http://owl.english.purdue.edu/handouts/research/r_apa.html

12. What is a bibliography?

As mentioned above, a reference list should contain *only* the material you have cited in your text. If other material as background reading has been used it may be included in a new list called the *Bibliography*. Format material in exactly the same way as in the reference section.

Endnotes

[1] The 4th edition of the APA Publication Manual distinguishes between copy manuscripts (i.e. those prepared for publication) and final manuscripts that will not be typeset, and the referencing conventions for the two types of manuscript differ. Student assignments and theses are produced in final copy form. The conventions presented in this chapter therefore relate to final manuscripts. If you are preparing manuscripts for publication in an APA journal, you will need to consult the APA Manual. *See* pp. 331–33 of the APA Manual (1995). For a copy manuscript, the first line of each entry is indented and subsequent lines are placed flush against the margin.

13

FORMAT FOR REFERENCES AND BIBLIOGRAPHY

References

American Psychological Association. (2001). *Publication Manual of the American Psychological Association* (5th ed.). Washington, DC: Author.

Ary, D., Jacobs, L.C., & Razavieh, A. (Eds). (1979). *Introduction to research in education*. New York: Holt, Rinehart and Winston.

Atkinson, R.C., & Shiffrin, R.M. (1971). The control of short-term memory. *Scientific American, 225*, 82–90.

Baddely, A. (1989). The uses of working memory. In P.R. Solomon, G.R. Goethals, C.M. Kelley and B.R. Stephens (Eds), *Memory: Interdisciplinary approaches*. New York: Springer-Verlag.

Bate, D., & Sharpe, P. (1990). *Student writer's handbook*. London: Harcourt and Brace Jovanovich Inc.

Brennan, M.C. (1990). *Style handbook: Department of Marketing*. Palmerston North: Business Studies Faculty, Massey University.

Brusaw, C.T., Alred, G.J., & W.E. Oliu. (1993). *The business writer's handbook* (4th ed.). New York, St Martin's Press.

Clancy, J., & Ballard, B. (1981). *Essay writing for students*. Melbourne: Longman Cheshire.

Crystal, D. (1988). *Rediscover grammar*. Essex: Longmans.

Department of English, Faculty of Humanities. (1994). *39.107 Applied English workbook*. Palmerston North: Massey University.

Flower, L. (1985). *Problem-solving strategies for writing* (2nd ed.). New York: Harcourt Brace Jovanovich.

Fluegelman, A., & Hewes, J.J. (1989). The wordprocessor and the writing process, pp.45–52. In Harty, K.J. (Ed.), *Strategies for business and technical writing*. San Diego: Harcourt Brace Jovanovich.

Morris, C.D., Bransford, J.D., & Franks, J.J. (1977). Levels of processing versus transfer appropriate processing. *Journal of Verbal Learning and Verbal Behavior, 16*, 519–533.

O'Shea, R. (1996). *Writing for Psychology* (2nd ed.). Sydney: Harcourt Brace.

Peterson, L.R., & Peterson, M.J. (1959). Short-term retention of individual verbal items. *Journal of Experimental Psychology, 58*, 193–198.

Sides, C.H. 1992: *How to write and present technical information* (2nd ed.). Cambridge, Cambridge University Press.

Sligo, F.X. (1994). *Effective communication in business* (2nd ed.). Palmerston North: Software Technology.

Weiten, W. (1992). *Psychology: Themes and variations* (2nd ed.). California: Brooks/Cole.

Bibliography

American Society for Horticultural Science. 1985. *ASHS publications manual*. Alexandria, American Society for Horticultural Science.

Cooper, H., & Hedges, L.V. (1994). *The handbook of research synthesis*. New York: Russell Sage Foundation.

Council of Biology Editors, Style Manual Committee. 1994. *Scientific style and format. The CBE manual for authors, editors and publishers* (6th ed.). Cambridge, Cambridge University Press.

Fox, D.J. (1969). *The research process in education*. New York: Holt Rinehart and Winston.

Gilbert, M.B. (1983). *Clear writing: A business guide*. New York: John Wiley and Sons Inc.

Jolly, J.M., Murray, D., & Keller, P.A. (1984). *How to write psychology papers*. Florida, USA: Professional Resource Exchange.

Kidder, L.H. (1981). *Research methods in social relations* (4th ed.). New York: Holt, Rinehart and Winston.

Lehmann, I.J., & Mehrens, W.A. (1979). *Educational research: Readings in focus* (2nd ed.). New York: Holt, Rinehart and Winston.

May, C. (1992). *Effective writing: a handbook for accountants* (3rd ed.). New Jersey: Prentice-Hall.

McMillan, B., & Meade, A. (1985). Observation: The Basic Techniques. *Set No 1* 1985: Item 7.

McCloskey, D.N. (1987). *The writing of economics*. New York: Macmillan.

Newby, M. (1989). *Writing: a guide for students*. Cambridge: Cambridge University Press.

New Zealand Government Printing Office. (1981). *Style book* (3rd ed.). Wellington Government Printer.

Orr, F. (1992). *Study skills for successful students*. St Leonards, Australia: Allen and Unwin.

Palmer, R. (1993). *Write in style*. London: E and F.N. Spon.

Porter, L.R., & Coggin, W. (1995). *Research strategies: In technical communication.* New York: Wiley and Sons.

Rosnow, R.L., & Rosnow, M. (1992). *Writing papers in psychology* (2nd ed.). Belmont, California: Wadsworth Publishing Company.

Smith, A. (1992). *Understanding children's development* (3rd ed.) Wellington: Bridget Williams Books.

Sternberg, R.J., & Rosnow, M. (1992). *The psychologist's companion.* New York: Cambridge University Press.

Strunk, W., & White, E.B. (1979). *The elements of style* (3rd ed.). New York: Macmillan.

Tallent, N. (1980). *Report writing in special education.* New Jersey: Prentice-Hall.

Tallent, N. (1983). *Psychological report writing* (2nd ed.). New Jersey, Prentice-Hall.

Turabian, K.L. (1996). *A manual for writers of term papers, theses and dissertations* (6th ed.). Chicago: University of Chicago Press.

Turk, C., & Kirkman, J. (1982). *Effective writing: Improving scientific, technical, and business communications.* New York: Chaucer Press.

Venolia, J. (1987). *Rewrite right!* Berkeley, California: Ten Speed Press.

Appendix A

USING MATERIAL FROM WRITTEN SOURCES

One of the main differences between assignments you may have written as a high-school student and academic assignments is the requirement that you place your argument or analysis within a scholarly context, that is, that you cite the ideas of other authors. Incorporating the ideas of other writers into your work is a new skill you need to learn when beginning tertiary studies if you are to achieve satisfactory grades.

1. Terminology

First of all, let's look at some terms that relate to using sources in your assignments.

1.1 Academic or Secondary Source

An academic source (or a secondary source) refers to any piece of material *produced by someone else* that you use when you are writing an assignment on a particular topic. This may include an article in a journal, an article in a newspaper, a book or a radio interview – anything that influences your discussion of a particular topic.

1.2 Quoting

A quotation is an exact copy of a passage from another source – it is a word-for-word transcript of someone else's words. If you use a quotation, you must indicate on your script that this is a quotation (by indenting the passage or putting it in inverted commas) and you must reference it correctly (for more detail on this, see Chapter 12, page 89).

1.3 Citing or Paraphrasing

Citing involves using someone else's ideas or data but expressing those ideas in your own words. For example, here is a quotation from Cliff Bunning's article Action Research: an Emerging Paradigm (1994, p. 37):

> The still emerging nature of action research leads it to appear disorganised and contradictory, because of the variety of approaches and beliefs adopted by the variety of practitioners and advocates of it.

You are writing an essay on the nature of action research and Bunning is one of the many authors that you have read on the subject. You want to include his ideas, but to present them fluently you choose to use your own words, that is, you choose to cite him. Here is one way you might do it:

Another difficulty Bunning (1994) identifies concerning action research is that it is not clearly developed and there is no consistent approach. Bunning attributes this lack of clarity to the fact that action research is still emerging as a methodology.

Note that when you cite information, you still need to acknowledge the source. Again, refer to Chapter 12 for more detail on how to reference citations.

1.4 Plagiarism

Plagiarism can be defined as:

Presenting the work of another as one's own work, including copying or paraphrasing, without acknowledging it as another person's work through full and accurate referencing. It applies to material presented through written, spoken, electronic, broadcasting, visual, performance or other medium.

Any form of plagiarism is considered to be Academic Misconduct and is viewed seriously by all tertiary institutions. You must take all warnings about plagiarism seriously: in some cases the consequences can involve failing your course or having the misdemeanour recorded on your academic record.

While a few students do cheat intentionally, many more plagiarise by accident, because they don't understand how to reference correctly or because they are careless with other sources. Make sure you read this Appendix and Chapter 13 very carefully to help avoid this mistake. Another very useful source of information is: http://owl. english.purdue.edu/owl/resource/589/01/.

Some courses use plagiarism detection systems such as Turnitin. You have nothing to worry about with these systems as long as you are careful to use correct referencing conventions.

2. When to reference citations

Referencing citations can cause problems for students: how do you decide what should be referenced? What if you are dealing with a very common and widely known issue? For example, you read in a book that 'communication is the lifeblood of the modern school system' and you want to express this idea in your assignment. But surely it is such a widely held view that it doesn't warrant referencing? Should you reference this idea?

If you are writing a report for a particular audience (for example, the chair of a commission investigating the needs of ESL students), you can answer this question simply: if the person you are writing for is likely to be generally familiar with the idea then you probably don't need to reference it.

However, an essay is more difficult to assess because your audience is not so clearly defined. Perhaps an analogy would help.

Imagine you are playing for a club cricket (or netball) team, and you are discussing strategies for an upcoming game with team-mates. Everyone in the group will know certain things: what the rules of the game are, what the names of the positions are, whether you are playing home or away. In the same way, when you are writing an essay in a particular discipline, certain pieces of knowledge are shared information. These do not need to be documented for the same reason that you do not take the time to explain to your team-mates what a wicket-keeper (or goal-keeper) is.

However, in your meeting, some things will be known only to one person. The captain may have played the opposing team before and remembers a weak player; another player may remember that the pitch tends to be slow, even in mid-summer. These ideas are expressed by single voices; they are not shared knowledge and so should be attributed to particular sources.

Documenting an essay works in the same way. For example, it is common knowledge amongst people working in education and social services that men and women use language differently. But few researchers have identified how men and women use language differently. If you find an author who does discuss specific differences or presents data showing, for example, that men interrupt more, then you would reference that source.

Once you become familiar with a subject area, you will develop a sense of what needs to be referenced. But, if you are in any doubt provide a reference; you are unlikely to be penalised for providing too many.

3. How to use sources

The next skill to develop is a judgement of how to use other authors in your work. Reports and essays use secondary sources quite differently.

3.1 Essays

A problem commonly raised by students is 'how much does my lecturer want to know about what *I* think, or do they just want to hear what everyone else has said?' It is an interesting question – and not easily answered and the best solution is to ask your lecturers some time.

Your lecturer, generally, does want to know what you think. But they want to know what you think in the context of the scholarly debate on the topic. In other words, they want to hear you play the solo instrument, but with the whole orchestra supporting you in the background.

An important point to realise is that there is an academic debate on every scholarly subject. Your marker wants you to position yourself within that debate. So, your essay should define the parameters and the points in between and where you stand in the debate (and why).

Let's use an example. You are writing an essay on the following topic:

> 'Affirmative action is required to ensure representation of
> women in senior positions within education services.'

As you read other writers on the topic, you find some people who feel that affirmative action is essential. Other writers state that affirmative action is condescending to women and prevents them from achieving recognition on their own merits. Still others suggest that affirmative action is useful in some contexts, but is a limited long-term strategy. Weighing up the evidence, you think it is a valuable short-term strategy in some contexts (e.g. X and Y) but alternative strategies (e.g. A and B) should also be employed.

The whole thrust of your essay, then, should be to explain and defend your position. But you should also explain who is on the perimeters of the debate and what the other positions are. If you have allied yourself with another writer, explain why you find their evidence so compelling and the others' limited.

To go back to our orchestral image: your proposition (and the defence of that proposition) is your solo; the orchestra is composed of the ideas of others, and all these parts, solo and orchestral, are vital to the work as a whole.

An essay asks for your informed view – in the light of others' views.

3.2 Reports

Because the purpose of a report is invariably practical (i.e. what should be done in a certain situation), you use the ideas of other authors to support your own practical observations.

e.g.

practical observation

back-up from another source

The school has grown so rapidly that its strategic plan (which was always vague and non-specific) is now almost totally irrelevant and inapplicable. Thus the institution lacks direction; as Gilbert *et al.* (1992) observe, a bad plan will cause the organisation to suffer.

Academic sources are used in the discussion section of your report to back up your practical analysis and solutions. They show the reader that you have some credibility, some authority and weight behind your statements. In the above example you are showing that you are not alone in thinking that poor planning can cause problems – other authorities have noted poor planning as a problem for other organisations.

4. Integration

Finally, a word about incorporating the ideas of others into your work: Remember that any assignment you write should be an integrated whole. Quotations and citations should be worked into your assignment so that they become an integral part of it.

Never leave a quotation to 'stand alone' or speak for itself. Introduce a quotation by letting the reader know your opinion of it: do you agree or disagree? Or do you feel that the author is only partially correct? Why? What are the limitations of this idea? How does this idea compare with someone else's? After the quotation, comment further or develop the idea in some way.

As your experience in writing academic assignments grows, and as your knowledge of the subject you are studying develops, you will find that incorporating the ideas of others fluently and elegantly into your own work becomes easier. Like all aspects of writing, this is a skill that develops with practice.

Appendix B

USING INFORMATION FROM OBSERVATION, INTERVIEWS AND JOURNALS

In collecting information for reports and research, educators often need to draw on information that relates to a particular child or specific context (e.g. home, classroom, playground or centre). Observations, interviews and journals are three common ways of collecting and recording information in education.

In recording observations, interviews or journal entries, you need to always make a note of relevant details, such as:

- time
- date
- setting
- brief details of relevant information about the subject
- brief details of the method(s) of observation or interviewing that you are using.

In keeping records and presenting data from observations, interviews or journals, you must keep ethical issues and issues of privacy in mind. The use of children's real names is obviously appropriate in terms of the usual assessment procedures undertaken as part of a classroom or centre program. However, for assignment and research purposes, the identity of participants (either adults or children) may need protection, and participants must be fully aware of the purpose and intended audience of your research.

If your assignment or research requires you to undertake observations or interviews that extend beyond what would be expected within the normal range of teaching duties, you may need to obtain written consent to do this from parents. You should clarify ethical issues with the lecturer who is supervising your assignment.

Observation

Systematic observation of children is a key tool in assessment and evaluation in education. There are many ways of undertaking observations, and your choice of method will depend on the type of information that you need and the time and resources that you have available.

The following observational methods are commonly used in educational settings.

Qualitative approaches

(i) Anecdotal recordings (sometimes called 'diary descriptions').
    Anecdotal recordings provide a brief description of the main features of an event. Anecdotal recordings are often used by parents or educators as a way of recording either typical instances of children's behaviour (e.g. what a child does as they watch a favourite TV program), or special events (e.g. a child's first steps). They are usually brief and easy to read. Although they tend to be informal, and reflect the observer's interests and biases, anecdotal recordings can provide interesting insights into children's behaviour.

(ii) Running records.
    We use running records to try to record everything that a child does during a set period of time. Very often a series of running records is used over an extended time span so that a detailed picture of a child's behaviour is built up. Running records can provide a rich source of information about children's behaviour and behaviour sequences. Traditionally, running records are made by writing down everything that the child does, and this can obviously be very demanding in terms of the observer's energy and attention. The use of video tape provides a useful method of recording the moment to moment behaviour of a child. Running records are usually analysed and coded after the observations have been undertaken.

Pre-coded, quantitative approaches

The following approaches are generally used when you want to focus on specific behaviour that you have identified before you undertake your observations. In using these methods of observation, you must identify exactly how you are going to define, or categorise, the behaviours that you are observing.

The results of these observations can often be usefully summarised in a graph, pie-chart or table.

(i)   Event or frequency recording: The number of times a specific behaviour or activity occurs.

(ii) Duration recording: The length of time spent engaged in a particular behaviour.

(iii) Interval recording: Observations made over an interval of time, then recorded and the process repeated over a length of time (e.g. 30 seconds observation; 30 seconds recording; therefore over a period of 15 minutes, 15 'interval recordings' will have been undertaken).

(iv) Time sampling: Observations made and recorded at specific times over a longer period of time (e.g. every 15 minutes).

(v)   Checklists: Sequenced lists of behaviour are checked off as they are observed. (Teachers often use checklist in conjunction with room on the page for qualitative comment on behaviour.)

(vi) Ratings scales: Behaviours are judged along a continuum, which is divided into a number of points that are assigned a numerical value.

The observational methods mentioned above are described in more detail in the following texts:

- Smith, A. (1992). *Understanding children's development* (3rd ed.) Wellington: Bridget Williams Books.
- McMillan, B. & Meade, A. (1985). *Observation: The Basic Techniques.* Set No 1, 1985: Item 7.

Interviews

Interviews can be an important source of information in educational research. The nature of your interview will be determined by the sort of information that you wish to collect and your relationship with the interviewee.

In setting up an interview, you should ensure your interviewee is as comfortable as possible. If you are using a recorder, make sure that your interviewee agrees to this and does not feel ill at ease being recorded. Ensure that your interviewee knows that they can refuse to answer any questions, or can request that an interview be terminated at any stage.

Careful planning of the questions that you wish to ask is essential. Some interviews are based on a set list of questions that have been worked out before the interview. Other interviews are less structured, and although there are certain areas that are pre-defined, the interview schedule (set of questions) is more flexible so that different leads can be followed up as appropriate during the interview. It is extremely important to prepare for interviews thoroughly, otherwise you will find that you have not used the opportunity to the full and have missed valuable or important information.

If you use a tape recorder, you may wish to transcribe the interview afterwards. However, this can be extremely time-consuming and you may find that it is possible to summarise most of the interview instead, transcribing only aspects of it that might be useful to quote in your research or report. Alternatively, you may be able to take adequate notes during the interview. This is more likely to be the case when you have a tightly structured list of questions. Finally, you may find that you can keep a record of your interview by making brief notes during the process and then expanding on these notes immediately afterwards.

Do not rely on your memory alone – and do write up interviews as soon as you can afterwards.

Journals

Journals are most commonly used in education as a means to encourage students and educators to reflect upon their own practice, identify their strengths, identify areas they wish to improve and monitor their progress in particular aspects of practice. In general, the focus of a journal is your own practice, behaviour and thoughts, rather than the behaviour of other learners or educators.

Journals are usually written up either at the end of a day or week. Your journal might focus on a specific aspect of your teaching, or might generally record your thoughts and reflections on what you have accomplished. Journal entries may also include feelings, interpretations and suggestions as well as descriptions of events that have occurred.

If you are required to keep a journal as part of a particular assignment, your assignment guidelines will provide more information about the sort of information that should be included in your journal entries. If you have chosen to use a journal as a method of collecting information for a research report, then the nature of the report and the information that you require will provide the basis for the type of journal entry that you keep. Journals can provide an invaluable record of what you have done as part of a research project. Depending on your own approach to your professional development, you may also find that journals can provide an extremely valuable tool for self-analysis and improvement.

Presenting data from observation, interviews and journal entries

In general you will include only a summary of your data within the body of your report or assignment. Quantitative data are often best summarised using graphs or tables (see Appendix E, Using graphics in reports, page 127). In summarising qualitative data, it is often useful to include excerpts from interviews or anecdotal or continuous recordings, to illustrate points that you wish to make. It is not customary to include all your data within the body of your assignment. However, it is often useful to include more extensive details of observations, copies of interview questionnaires, and transcripts of interviews and journal entries as appendices to your report or research.

Remember that you are working with human beings.

Appendix C

PRESENTING A SEMINAR

1. Introduction

At some time most students and professionals are required to speak to an audience. This may be the presentation of a research paper, a theoretical report, advice to parents – there are many possibilities.

Seminars give students the opportunity to present information to an audience and, more importantly, also provide the opportunity for feedback. Seminars are not lecture presentations – they are designed to generate questions and discussion.

To some people, speaking in public comes relatively easily, while for others having to face an audience is a truly nerve-wracking experience. However, even the most experienced public speakers are often anxious, keyed-up and nervous before they begin speaking. This is a normal human reaction ('stage fright' is a severe form), the fear usually being a result of your desire to do well and have a rapport with the audience.

To overcome this nervousness, the experienced speaker:
* is thoroughly prepared
* is positive
* knows the audience (who are they? what are their needs?)
* talks confidently and enthusiastically
* speaks slowly (uses short sentences)
* uses eye contact
* uses pauses
* uses aids purposefully (PowerPoint slides, acetates, etc.)
* concludes firmly and confidently
* practises.

This guide offers a few suggestions that may assist you. There is no single correct way to give a seminar; each person has their own individual style. Nevertheless, there are a few general rules you should consider carefully before deciding to break them and a few pitfalls to avoid at all costs. Hopefully, the ideas here will help you to make a clearer presentation, keep the audience interested and perhaps even encourage you to enjoy yourself!

Make your point clearly.

2. Planning

This stage is the key. There are one or two people in every hundred who can talk for 30-40 minutes about a topic in an organised, understandable way at a moment's notice. Another 10 or so have the confidence to try, but should never have done so. Most of us need to prepare very carefully.

Seminars must have a beginning, a middle and an end. Very obvious? It is amazing how many seminars are given where the presenter plunges straight into the body of the seminar without warning, or suddenly stops without presenting any general discussion or conclusion.

2.1 The Introduction

The introduction should clearly set out the scope and importance of the topic. It needs to:
- explain why the topic is an issue or a problem and why it is important
- briefly summarise any necessary background information (context), historical details, specialist terminology, etc.

- give the audience an idea of what you intend to discuss with a clear statement of the objectives or the aspects of the study you intend covering in the presentation.

2.2 The body of the seminar

Here the essentials of your topic are presented along with the information/results you obtained. Your findings/arguments are then discussed.
- Focus clearly on your topic.
- Do not present information you don't intend to discuss.
- Build up your story slowly and logically.
- Recap if the story becomes a complicated one.
- Aim to keep the audience with you.

2.3 Conclusions

Finally, discuss the implications of the information you have presented, your own ideas and what you think it all means.

3. Preparation

Having planned what you are going to say, spend some time considering how you are going to present it. What visual aids are you going to use? Plan them with the audience in mind, remembering that most of them will not have had any experience of your topic. If you do this carefully, visual aids can make the seminar much easier for the audience to follow and much easier for you to present.

Most people will use PowerPoint slides and sometimes overhead projection (OHP) sheets. There are some clear guidelines here:
- Use legible, large text. Make sure your font size is appropriate to the size of the room you will present in.
- Be as professional as you can – untidy slides are distracting and difficult to read.
- Look at the slide when it goes up on the screen. Check the audience can see what you want them to see.
- Explain the details of your figure or table.
- Pause and give people time to look at your slide.
- Check how to work the equipment before the seminar!
- Do not block the screen by standing in the line of vision.
- Do not put too much information on one slide – just point to key ideas.

- Do not include unnecessary information.
- Summarise the main point(s) of each slide as you show it.

Remember:	1.	Each slide you show should have a purpose, and you should help the audience recognise what that purpose is.
	2.	Don't inflict 'death by PowerPoint'! Not everything you say must also be on screen.

4. Types of delivery

There are four possible ways to deliver a presentation.

1. Manuscript method

Read directly from prepared text; not recommended for a seminar presentation because it becomes monotonous and there is no contact with the audience, who will quickly become inattentive.

2. Memory method

Memorise the entire presentation; not recommended for a seminar presentation because of the danger of memory loss!

3. Impromptu method

No preparation, make it up as you go along; not recommended for a seminar presentation because you are wasting everyone's time!

4. Extemporaneous method

Using an outline, key phrases or brief notes; recommended for a seminar presentation because it has the advantages of good eye contact, naturalness of language, rhythm, pace and voice modulation.

5. Timing a seminar

Planning your seminar so it does not go on too long can often be a problem. If you do not have much experience in this, careful rehearsal is the only answer. Remember that in a rehearsal it is very easy to go much faster than you should in front of an audience. Make sure you are clear about how much time you have available for your actual presentation, and how much you are expected to leave for questions and discussion.

You may find it useful to put check timings on your notes to make sure you are not running over time too much.

- Do not keep to time by speeding up your presentation.
- Do not keep to time by leaving out your conclusion.

As a safeguard it is often a good idea to have some optional material prepared that can be left out if, on the day, you find that you are running over time. If you find yourself in this situation make sure you leave the optional item out completely – do not skip through it very quickly and confuse your audience.

6. Pause, poise and presence of mind

Remember that pauses when using visual aids help your audience – they get time to assimilate and understand what you are saying. Try to keep an eye on the audience and check that they appear to be following you. Pay particular attention to those who looked enthusiastic and interested at the start. Reference to these people will give you confidence if they continue to look interested as the seminar progresses.

Pauses can help you too. They can help you relax, collect your thoughts and think carefully about what you are going to say next.

Apart from this, confidence comes from the knowledge that you have prepared as best you can and that you know and understand your material well.

7. Handling questions at the end of the seminar

- Listen carefully.
- If you do not understand the question, don't guess. Ask the questioner to repeat what he or she said.
- If you still do not understand, ask the seminar chairperson for help.
- If you have no idea of the answer, say so immediately! Do not waffle.
- There is no substitute for good preparation and good understanding of your topic.

8. Summary and helpful hints

8.1 Before your Seminar

- Practise beforehand (days if possible) – practice does make perfect!
- Make sure you can pronounce all the words.

- Make sure you are thoroughly prepared, and that any aids are understandable, can be seen from the back of the room and that you can use them effectively.
- Look your best – looking good helps you feel good, which helps your confidence.
- Be aware of your distracting mannerisms (e.g. pen clicking, saying 'ah' or 'um' every 15 seconds). What can you do to control them?
- Keep jargon and technical words to an absolute minimum.
- Anticipate questions – think of some answers beforehand if possible.

8.2 During your Presentation

- Communicate first – keep your mind on your message.
- Keep to the point – do not waffle.
- Speak clearly but not too slowly.
- Talk to everyone in your audience (not the floor or a spot on the back wall); make eye contact.
- Use open gestures; try to look relaxed; do not pace up and down.
- If you think a pause is required, use silence, not 'ums' and 'ahs'.
- Keep to time.

DIRECTIVE FOR LULLING AN AUDIENCE TO SLEEP

Wear a dark suit and conventional tie; turn down the lights; close the curtains; display a crowded slide and leave it in place; stand still; read your paper without looking up; read steadily with no marked changes in cadence; show no pictures; use grandiloquent words and long sentences.

(Booth 1993)

Appendix D

PARAGRAPHING, PUNCTUATION AND PRETENTIOUSNESS: ELEMENTS OF STYLE

What is said and the way it is said can be equally important determinants of a successful assignment. This section focuses on three key elements of academic writing – paragraphing, punctuation and appropriate academic style.

1. Paragraphing

Paragraphing technique can be the factor that distinguishes between a page of muddled ideas and a page of reasoned, logical prose. It is wise to stick to a simple paragraphing style when writing at an undergraduate level, where clarity of thinking and presentation are vitally important. The following principles should guide the way for paragraphs that are written for undergraduate assignments.

1.1 Every paragraph should contain a single developed idea

Paragraphs are the building blocks of an assignment. If each paragraph develops one idea fully, the reader will have the opportunity to read and consider one idea at a time. If there is more than one idea in a paragraph, the reader is likely to be confused – or may miss one of the ideas.

1.2 The key idea of the paragraph should be stated in the opening sentence of the paragraph

This is called using a deductive paragraphing style. Because readers' attention tends to be most focused at the beginning of a chunk of writing, it seems sensible to state a key idea at the beginning of a paragraph. This key idea is called a topic sentence. The rest of the sentences can then develop, explain and support the topic sentence. It is a good idea to write the topic sentence in your own words rather than using a quotation.

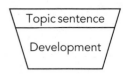

1.3 Use a variety of methods to develop your topic sentences

There are many ways to develop an idea. Here are a few of them. Note that each paragraph example is written in a deductive style (i.e. the topic sentence comes first).

Develop your topic sentences using:

Descriptive or factual details

This method of paragraph development involves giving a more thorough, concrete explanation of the idea expressed in a general way in the topic sentence. Factual details give measurable, observable or historical information that can be verified. Descriptive details give specific characteristics of the subject being discussed.

> e.g. Planning is a vital aspect of the management of every school. It gives a school direction and a sense of purpose. It draws all members of the school community (parents, staff, the Board, students) together and makes every decision clearer. Without planning, a school may founder either through lack of direction or through divisive directions.

Illustrations and examples

The writer may use several brief examples or one extended illustration. The illustration may be factual or hypothetical (invented for the purpose of illustration).

> e.g. Planning is a vital aspect of every school. For Foothill High School in Wakari, planning was a lifesaver. In 1998 the school was facing a declining roll, truancy and behaviour problems and a general feeling of malaise. There was no direction in the school and the staff, exhausted by daily control problems, had all the energy and focus of frontline troops after a bloody battle. Sonya Cahill was appointed Principal in 2001. Her first step was to draw all the staff together to construct a new mission and plan for the school. A decision was taken to develop a new integrated studies program and an extensive music focus. Clear operational plans were developed to deal with daily control problems. Within five years the school roll was full and growing. The school staff, Board, students and parents – had a new energy and life.

Definitions

These can be used to explain concepts or terms that may be unfamiliar to the reader. It is generally more effective to attempt your own definition rather than copying out of a dictionary. A definition is often more effective when combined with an illustration or example.

> e.g. Planning is vital to all schools. Planning is a broad term. It involves many processes – forming a mission statement, designing a strategic plan, defining goals and establishing operational methods. It has implications for every level of the school community.

Authority

Finally, it is common to use authority to develop the topic sentence. This is appropriate and useful because it positions your work within an academic debate – it shows that your idea is supported by people who may have more credibility and standing than you do.

> e.g. Planning is vital to all schools. Sanders (2003) sees it as 'the skeleton of the school, determining its structure and capabilities' (p. 16). Other researchers (Canton, 2002; Fiach & Paine, 2005) emphasise its capacity to create a sense of direction and unity.

1.4 Finally, use connectives between and within paragraphs to unify your writing

A series of unconnected ideas can be confusing for a reader. In most academic writing, every sentence or paragraph should be logically connected to the sentence or paragraph that precedes or follows it. Your reader should not have to struggle to work out what the connection is. Instead you should use connectives to make the relationships between your ideas very clear. Connectives can be a single word (e.g. however, because, therefore) or a phrase (e.g. 'Because of the nature of this development …' or, 'Despite the consequences of such behaviour …').

Following is a list of short connectives that will help you to clarify the development of your ideas to your reader. Try to vary your connectives – if you always use 'however' to indicate a change of direction, your writing style could appear repetitive and uninteresting. Four types of logical relationships are set out in the following list.

LOGICAL CONNECTIVE EXAMPLES	
To add to an idea	also, in similar ways, in addition, likewise, moreover, similarly, furthermore
To change direction	however, despite this, instead, nevertheless, on the other hand, still, alternatively
To develop beyond an idea	therefore, as a result, accordingly, because of this, hence, consequently, thus
To illustrate	for example, for instance, specifically, to illustrate

2. Punctuation

2.1 The full stop or period

This is used to mark the end of a sentence. It may be replaced by the question mark (?) or the exclamation mark (!).

- Have you ever wondered why leaves fall off trees in the autumn?
- It is very important to use punctuation correctly! Think of what would happen if you didn't! Readers might be misled! Don't risk it! Attend a lecture on punctuation today!

2.2 The comma

This is used to mark off bits of a longer sentence to make meaning clearer.
1. Joining two sentences with a conjunction:
    - I came out to Massey, and I went to my lecture.
    - I tried to get some milk, but the dairy had sold out.
2. Where you have added bits to the basic sentence:
    (a) as openers:
        - However, I got some at the supermarket.
        - In the end, I borrowed some from my flatmate.
    (b) in the middle, usually between the subject and verb:
        - The baby, who had cried all night, went to sleep at dawn.
        - My only transport, a brand new mountain bike, was stolen yesterday.
    (c) as enders:
        - The baby went to sleep at dawn, to his parents' relief.
        - I borrowed some socks from my flatmate, that generous soul.

3. To list items in a series:
   - I am studying German, English, philosophy and history.
   - Whether you are singing, playing an instrument or dancing, expressing yourself with music is relaxing and energising.
4. Writing addresses or large numbers, or any other potentially confusing situation:
   - 235B Ponsonby Road North, Auckland (could be Ponsonby Road, North Auckland).
   - NZ$3,000,000.

2.3 The semicolon

This has two common uses.
1. Joining two complete sentences that are closely related, or that reflect each other:
   - We all enjoy our flat; it has a great atmosphere.
   - There are the benefits of sharing; there is also the disadvantage of lack of privacy.
2. Listing complex items that need commas in themselves:
   - When leaving New Zealand you should have a current passport, issued by your own government; a re-entry permit, which you can apply for at the Immigration Department; travellers cheques, obtainable at your bank; and a good book, which you can buy at the airport before you leave.

2.4 The colon

This is a clue that something is coming, a sort of introductory flourish. You will probably use it in two situations.
1. To introduce a quote of more than one sentence:
   - Wolf (1993, p. 190) sees this situation as complex:
     We are all struggling against impulses that draw us backwards, and compensate psychologically for the strangeness of a great leap forward. The backlash wasn't generated just by men; part of the stasis women experience derives from their own ambivalence about entering the alien land of equality.
2. To introduce a smaller quote if it says what you have just said in different words:
   - The situation is no better in England, according to Wolf: 'The same absence of women on political discussion programs in Britain was noted by *The Independent*' (Wolf, 1993, p. 89).

3. To introduce a list:
    - Only a few basic ingredients are needed to make scones: flour, baking powder, butter and milk.

2.5 The apostrophe

This seems to be the most difficult punctuation mark to use correctly, but there are really only two main uses for it.

1. To indicate that letters have been left out of a word:

    won't (will not)
    I'll (I will)
    shan't (shall not)
    we'll (we shall or we will)
    I'd (I would or I had)
    you'd (you had)
    it's (it is – compared to its in (iii) below)

Apostrophes are not yet extinct.

2. To indicate possession:
    (a)   for singular nouns, add 's:

the man's name	the child's toy
the student's room	a cat's dinner
Mary's film	a girl's birthday

(b)   for plural nouns formed by adding s, just add ':
the students' flat   all girls' uniforms
four cats' dinners   both Marys' mothers

(c)   for plural nouns formed in other ways, add 's:
men's names   children's toys
women's clothing

(d)   for words that already have lots of s sounds, just add ':
Rameses' monument   Jesus' words
scissors' blade

There is **no need for an apostrophe** in these situations:

(i)   reference to decades, as in the 1860s, or the 1920s.

(ii)   when making a plural of a word ending in a vowel.
Tomatoes, potatoes and bananas are perfectly all right, but some
greengrocers seem driven to write tomato's, potato's and banana's.

(iii)   the possessive of a pronoun, as in ours, yours, hers and its
(meaning 'belonging to it' – compare with – it's in 1. above).

REMEMBER:

it's	means	it is	– letter left out
its	means	belonging to it	– no apostrophe

2.6 The dash

This is used like a comma, but gives greater emphasis. It may be used singly or in a pair.
Try to avoid using this too often; it gives the prose a choppy feel.

- We all got there eventually – and then it was time to leave.
- We take turns – at least we try to – at shopping and cooking.

2.7 The bracket

Again, this is used to mark off a thought that is relevant but not crucial to the sentence.
It is less emphatic (smoother) than the dash.

- My mother worked for a legal firm (which has since been sold) on the corner of
Featherston Street.
- The landlord is always coming around (to check up, we suspect), so we are
looking for another flat.

Note the comma that is needed between 'around' and 'so' is after the bracket (see the first rule of commas, above). Never put a comma before a bracket!

2.8 The ellipsis

This indicates that something has been left out of a quote, or, occasionally, it is put in for effect at the end of a sentence – usually an indication that the writer has left something out for you to fill in.

- 'Management ... is a major component ...' (Rice, 1991, p. 17).
- Then, just as John saw the lights of his house clearly, a large shadow moved between him and his goal, and he felt a damp, clammy arm pull him inexorably towards a reeking, drooling mouth…

2.9 The hyphen

This small punctuation mark can be very useful to tie together two words and avoid confusion.

- A Dutch-cheese importer is anyone who imports Dutch cheese; a Dutch cheese importer is a Dutch person who imports any sort of cheese.
- A small-arms retailer will sell you a hand-gun; a small arms retailer is a physically small person who sells a wide range of guns.

Quoted material from:

Wolf, N. (1993). *Fire with fire: The new female power and how it will change the 21st century.* London: Chatto & Windus Ltd.

Style

Now for a few words about the style of academic writing. Style is a difficult issue to define and explain. Remember that even in academic writing the main concern should be to communicate your ideas clearly to a reader. Style therefore, should be designed on the basis of three things:

- the nature of your message
- the purpose of the sender
- the needs of the reader.

Most academic writing at an undergraduate level (essays in particular) should be aimed at an audience that is intelligent but not well-informed on your subject.

In particular, these guidelines should be followed.

- Sentences should be short, and they should contain a single idea.
- Write in the active voice.
- Cut out any unnecessary words.
- Do not use personal pronouns (I, we, you) unless you are told you can.
- If there is a choice between a long word and a short word, choose the short word.
- If jargon is used, define the terms.
- Use gender neutral and culturally safe language.
- Be direct.
- Aim for clarity.

The last point is perhaps the most important, and incorporates many of the other items on the list. Do not make the mistake of thinking that complex sentences, a pretentious, convoluted style and long Latinate words will impress the reader. Such a style is more likely to obscure your ideas. Write in a simple, clear, yet formal manner, using language that you fully understand, and you will communicate with the reader.

Appendix E

USING GRAPHICS IN REPORTS

Using graphics in your reports is an excellent way of focusing your audience's attention on the points you are making and presenting your points in a manner that is easy for your audience to understand. But, as graphics are also a great way to confuse or inadvertently mislead your audience, it is important that you know which type of graphic is appropriate to use, when to use it and how to use it. The rules and points of style that we will introduce you to in this Appendix are fairly general and are designed to get you started and confident in what you are doing. If your department requires you to follow a specific style, then refer to the appropriate style manual.

There are two types of graphics: tables and figures. Tables are best suited to displaying specific, related facts, data or statistics in a small space. You can present data more concisely in tables than you can in text, and more accurately than you can achieve with figures. Detailed comparisons among different groups within the data are often easier to display in a table than in a figure, and nearly always easier to express than in text. On the other hand, figures are an excellent method of displaying trends, general comparisons, movements, distributions and cycles in your data.

Before introducing you to some of the finer points of tables and figures, let's pause to affirm the overarching principle of their use in all forms of writing.

> **SIMPLY STATED:**
> Graphics should document or clarify, but not duplicate, data given in text or other graphics.

This means that you should never present a graph and a table of the same set of data, or give a verbatim description in your text of data that you have also presented in a graphic. Understand, however, that your text and graphics are not independent. A characteristic of good writers is their ability to link the graphics with their text, using their text to highlight, interpret and discuss the information in the graphics. If you remember nothing else in this Appendix, remember this point: graphics and text should work together to provide clear information to the reader.

1. Using tables

1.1 Informal tables

Books on writing style usually distinguish between two types of tables – *informal* and *formal*. An informal table is a simple list. Informal tables are physically separated from the text by at least one empty line above and below the table and often by additional margin space on both sides of the table. It is this separation that sets informal tables apart from the text and gives them their visual attraction and attention from your audience. Unlike formal tables (as you will soon see), informal tables do not have headings (titles) nor are they numbered. Usually, each line of the informal table will be bulleted.

For example, if we were to summarise the main characteristics of informal tables in an informal table, we would note that informal tables are:

- separated from the main text by white space
- displayed without any headers or number
- bulleted (although this is an optional extra)
- just simple lists.

1.2 Formal tables

At first, you may not like constructing formal tables, because they require more effort to build than simple informal tables. But do persevere in developing this skill, because the value of formal tables for presenting complex information concisely, accurately and clearly more than compensates for the extra effort required in their construction. But before you expend the effort, make sure you decide whether or not a formal table is appropriate.

Use the following checklist to decide when a formal table is appropriate:

- You have more than six items of data to present. You can usually express in your text the relationships and meaning inherent in small numbers of data (i.e. less than six items) without having to resort to creating a table.
- There are more than two outcomes in your data. For example, if some student groups 'passed' oral examinations while other groups 'failed', such information is better presented in your text.
- Your data actually contains important information. It is pointless, for example, to set up a table to present data that is not statistically significant in its magnitude. Tables are not the place to archive data (no matter how much time you took to collect and collate it!).

The communicative value of a table depends on how well you link it with your text. It is *not* sufficient to just create a table without providing any reference to it in your text. Link your table to your text through an *interpretative translation* of the data in your table. In an interpretative translation, you discuss the highlights and interpret the main points of the table within a wider discussion of what the information in the table means to the topic of your report. Guide your readers through your table, but don't make the common mistake of literally repeating, in words, the content of the table. Vary the approach you make in linking your table to your text. It quickly becomes very tedious for your audience if they repeatedly meet such phrases as 'Table 1 shows that distributed practice resulted in fewer errors than did massed practice'. Instead, use alternative phrases to achieve the link, e.g. 'Distributed practice resulted in fewer errors than massed practice (Table 1)'.

1.3 Building your table

Setting up a table so that the data is readily comprehensible to your audience is simple as long as you remember a guiding principle of table construction:

> Organise the data so that the most important elements read down, not across.

Before explaining this by way of example, let's first refresh your memory of the basic anatomy of a formal table. The five basic skeletal components or sections of a formal table are displayed in the following graphic, with Table 1 showing these components 'fleshed out'.

The number of the table and its title always appear at the top of the table.	
The boxhead contains the column headings.	
The stub column(s) lists, row by row, the categories about which the information is being presented.	The data being presented appears in columns in the body of the table.
Footnotes go in this section.	

Figure E.1: Basic anatomy of a formal table

In Table 1, the stub column contains the group (girls and boys) and learning disability (with or without) variables. The body contains the data on the number of observations in each group and the number of correct responses to the tests. Notice how footnotes in the table are used to present points of clarification of the makeup of the data in the table.

Table 1 Mean number of correct responses on verbal tests[a] of children with and without learning disabilities, and in different forms.

			Form		
Group		n[b]	2	4	6
Girls	With	17	240	256	272
	Without	24	285	295	310
Boys	With	24	232	247	265
	Without	25	281	289	306

[a] Maximum score = 320
[b] Numbers of children out of 25 in each group who completed the tests.

What are the other important features you should note about this table?
- The title is at the top of the table.
- The constrained use of lines.
- Each row and column title starts with a capital letter
- There is white space in the table – the data are not cramped together.
- The data in the columns in the body of the table are equally spaced.

Now, let's get back to the issue of table construction. First, look again at Table 1. Notice how it is very easy to compare the test performance among forms for any combination of gender and learning disability. Now look at Table 2.

Table 2 Mean number of correct responses on verbal tests[a] of children with and without learning disabilities, and in different forms.

		Learning disability	
Group		With	Without
Girls	Form 2	240	285
	Form 4	256	295
	Form 6	272	310
	n[b]	17	24
Boys	Form 2	232	281
	Form 4	247	289
	Form 6	265	306
	n[b]	24	25

[a] Maximum score = 320
[b] Numbers of children out of 25 in each group who completed the tests.

This table contains the same information as Table 1, but the layout is designed to aid comparison between the presence and absence of a learning disability on test performance for any combination of gender and form. The important point to recognise in both these examples is that it is easier to compare numbers in adjacent columns than numbers in adjacent rows. This means that you must carefully consider what the important comparisons are that you want to present to your audience.

2. Using figures

Although the term *figure* can refer to a photograph, flow-chart, map or diagram, we will focus on the most common type of figure, the graph. Quite simply, graphs present numerical data in visual form. Graphs are excellent devices to show trends or important patterns in your data; or to compare the relative responses of different groups (e.g. boys and girls, ethnic groups) to some factor (e.g. a test). Remember, however, that if the data itself is important, then present it in a table; you should not expect your audience to read data off the axes of a graph. The three main types of graph you are most likely to use are *line* graphs, *bar* graphs and *pie* graphs.

2.1 Line Graphs

You should use a line graph whenever you want to show the changes in the level or response of some variable (e.g. a test score) against some form of continuous variable (e.g. age, calendar date, sequence). Line graphs are particularly useful for comparing the relationship between two or more groups of data (Figure E.2).

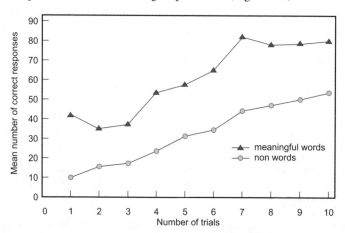

Figure E.2: Mean number of correctly recalled non words and meaningful words over 10 sequential trials. Each point is the mean of n=15 observations.

There are several points to notice in this example of a line graph:

- The vertical (y) and horizontal (x) axes have simple, clear labels.
- The axis labels run parallel with the axes.
- A simple font type (sans serif; e.g. Helvetica, Arial) is used.
- The unit of measurement (i.e. mean number) of the variable plotted on the vertical axis is clearly presented in the label. The two data sets (i.e. meaningful words and non words) are distinguished from each other by the use of different symbols. You could use different coloured lines or different styles of lines (e.g. a solid line and a dashed or dotted line) to achieve the same purpose.
- A key for the distinguishing features is included in the graph.
- The title appears at the bottom of the graph.
- As well as the description of the graph, the title contains points of clarification of the data. (Compare this style to that of tables where such information is contained in the footnote section.)

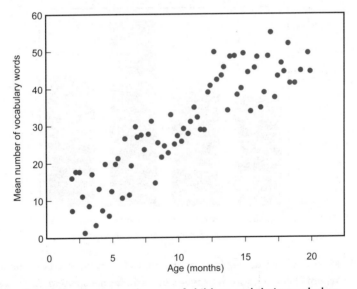

Figure E.3: Correlation between the age of children and their vocabulary.

A common version of the line graph is the scattergram (Figure E.3). Use scattergrams to illustrate the general relationship between pairs of measured variables. In these graphs, you are trying to show your audience whether the relationship is linear (as in Figure E.3) or curved (curvilinear). As a consequence, the points are not joined together.

2.2 Bar Graphs

You'll find bar graphs very useful for presenting categorical data (i.e. data measured from separate groups of 'things' such as groups of people, types of response and brands of goods). Bar graphs share many style characteristics of line graphs: their vertical and horizontal axes are simply and clearly labelled; the units of measure are presented; and the title appears below the figure (Figure E.4). In this example, the categories are the types of instructional training.

Bar graphs are ideal for comparing the response of categories within categories (Figure E.5). When you use bar graphs for this purpose, take time to identify the categories important to your comparison. For example, in Figure E.5a the major category is 'types of instructional training' and gender is the minor category; these roles are reversed in Figure E.5b. Notice the major change in appearance of the graphs, even though the same data set is being used.

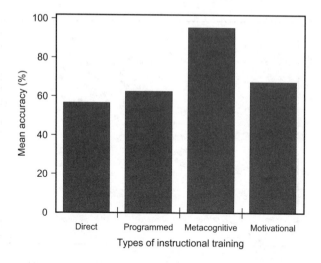

Figure E.4: Mean accuracy scores for a mathematics test conducted on primary school children under four types of instructional training. Data are pooled over gender.

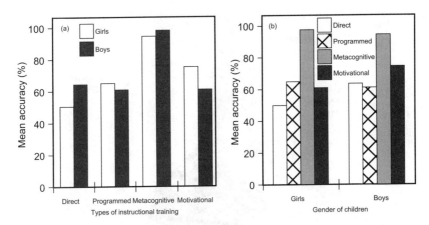

Figure E.5: Mean accuracy scores for a mathematics test conducted on primary school children under four types of instructional training. (Note: these data are fictitious and are used solely for illustration of the effect of choice of the major category in multi-factor data sets.)

2.3 Pie Graphs

Whenever you need to compare percentages of a whole, then a pie graph (pie chart) is the graph to use (Figure E.6). Provided that you don't have too many wedges (i.e. categories), pie graphs are easy to interpret, and have a strong visual impact.

The rules of style associated with these graphs are as simple as the graphs themselves:

- Make the relative percentages clear by starting at the 12 o'clock position and sequence the wedges clockwise.
- Sequence the wedges from largest to smallest (although sometimes this isn't possible because it is difficult to clearly present the labels of small wedges adjacent to each other).
- Give the percentage value of each wedge, either inside each wedge or as part of the label.
- Keep all the labels horizontal.

2.4 Graphics Abuse

Look out for these pitfalls. First, many graphics packages (particularly those associated with spreadsheet packages) offer you *line* and *X-Y* graphs. Line graphs differ from *X-Y* graphs in the way in which the levels of the variable on the horizontal axis are displayed.

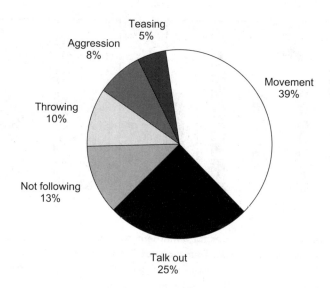

Figure E.6: Percentage of intervals in which disruptive behaviours occurred during study conditions. (Note: these data are fictitious.)

In line graphs, the levels are always equally spaced, regardless of their magnitude; in X-Y graphs, the spacing accurately reflects the magnitude of the level. Thus, if your horizontal axis is time (e.g. 1, 2, 5, 12, and 13 weeks), these will appear as equal spacing (incorrect) on a line graph and arithmetically spaced (correct) on an X-Y graph.

Second, keep your graphs as simple and uncluttered as possible. Many (spreadsheet) graphics packages, by default, produce grid lines at each major point on the vertical and horizontal axes. Such lines should be 'turned off' because they generally clutter up the graph, distracting your audience from the important information in the graph. Similarly, don't be seduced by the wide range of fancy variations of the basic types of graphs that are available in many graphics packages. For example, unless 3D bars actually improve the message of your bar graph, then don't use them (even if they are the default setting!).

Third, the default (and often the only) position for the title of the graph in many (software) graphics packages is at the top of the graph. This position is not acceptable style for the reports you will write. Consequently, you will have to use your word-processor to produce the title and description of your graphs in the correct position below the graph!

Many computers allow you to print (wrap) text around one or both sides of your tables and figures. Just because the software allows this doesn't mean that this is appropriate style. And for most, if not all, of the reports that you will prepare for your courses, wrapping text around tables and figures is not appropriate style.

Be honest with your figures. We all know that 'a picture is worth a thousand words', but don't forget that a picture can hide a hundred 'truths'. Look at Figure E.7a that plots the academic performance of children from different European countries. It appears as though there are considerable differences in performance between the different groups. Now look at Figure E.7b. This graph shows the same set of data but against a different scale on the vertical axis. The differences among the groups now appear marginal. Which figure do you think gives a clearer picture of the results?

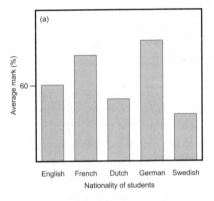 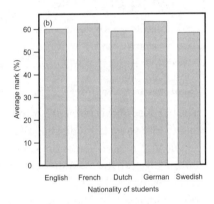

Figure E.7: Academic performance of students of different nationality in their first year of university study. (Note: these data are fictitious and used solely for illustration of the dangers of exaggerated scales (a) compared with normal scales (b).)

Remember!

A final word about graphics (and yes, we have already mentioned this point, but it's important!). Remember that your audience deserves some guidance with your tables and figures. Don't follow the bad habit of many writers who lead their audience to a table or figure with a phrase such as 'The influence of the change in curriculum on truancy levels is shown in Table 2 and Figure 1', and then move on to the next point. Don't leave your audience hanging on your graphics; guide them into the data. Tell your audience what you think the data have revealed. Remember that you are writing a report, not a crossword; your aim is to give a clear description, not to drop clues.

Appendix F

EXAM SKILLS

Identifying probable exam topics

To read notes, textbooks and study guides over and over again is not the best way to prepare for exam essays. It is important that you try to identify and prepare topics, key themes and/or issues that will probably be set. To do this:

- ***Read through the notes you have made***

  The purpose of this is to refresh your memory about the content of the paper and to give you a fair indication of the probable scope of the exam paper. This should also remind you of the key concepts and issues that have been covered during the year, the main divisions into which the covered materials fit, and the rationale underlying the whole paper. Note in particular the extent to which certain topics and sections have been covered – this is usually a good indication of their importance and the likelihood of them turning up in the exam. Note also the emphasis placed on these topics/sections by your lecturers (or in your study guides).

- ***Look at past exam papers***

  You do this to identify the topics/themes/issues that are usually covered and to become familiar with the format of the exam. Make sure, however, that you are aware of any changes to lecturers, paper content, and/or exam format that may have occurred since these previous exam papers were set.

  Of course, you can never really be certain that a particular topic will turn up, and it is very difficult to predict the precise wording and focus of the actual questions you will get in the exam. Therefore:

- ***Always prepare more topics than will be required in the exam***

  For example, if you have to write four essays in the exam, prepare at least six topics. And make sure that you are at least reasonably familiar with the other topics, themes, and issues covered in the paper even if you do not prepare for them thoroughly – just in case.

- *Prepare your essay topics comprehensively*

What this means is that you should prepare to the extent that you are more or less certain you will be able to answer any question on the topic irrespective of wording or focus.

Preparation and revision activities

- *As noted earlier, prepare likely topics, key themes and/or issues.*

- *Collect and summarise all relevant information on the topic:*

This includes definitions, factual statements, evidence, examples, opinions, descriptions and other similar information. You collect these mainly from your notes, but also (if necessary) from your study guides, texts, assigned readings, handouts and other relevant sources.

- *Organise the information you have collected:*

Structure these under theme headings such as: definitions/descriptions, supporting evidence, strengths/weaknesses, applications/limitations, similarities/differences, and so on.

- *Make written summaries and/or construct 'mind maps' of the points and information you have gathered and organised.*

- *Check the material you have revised against past exam papers:*

In doing this, examine which questions relate to the material you have been revising. Try to get a clear understanding of what points you would need to cover in order to answer each relevant question.

- *Try framing your own exam questions:*

As you learn and understand better the materials you are revising, you will probably start getting some ideas about questions that are likely to be asked for each topic. See if you can quickly jot down important points and other information you would include in your answers should these questions be asked.

- *Write trial answers to some questions:*

  Especially if you have time, you may find it very useful to try writing answers to some questions (e.g. ones you have thought up or ones from previous exam papers) without looking at your notes and within the time limit of the exam. If you are short of time, just write these trial answers in note form – paying attention particularly to the relevant and important points you would include (and can/cannot remember) and the way you would structure your answers. Some lecturers and tutors may be willing to skim through these trial efforts and comment on your performance. Comments from other students may also be helpful. But the greatest value of writing trial answers is getting practice in doing what you will be doing in your exams (namely: thinking, remembering, writing, structuring, etc.). It will also give you a fair idea of how much you can write on a question within a given time limit.

- *If you have an open book exam, organise well your materials beforehand:*

  This is important so that you can use them quickly and efficiently within the time constraints of the exam. So make sure your notes will be easy to use, and that you will be able to find relevant things quickly in your texts (put markers), and so on.

What to aim for in essay exams

- Clarity of focus on the set topic (i.e. answer the question given).
- Comprehensive coverage of the central issues directly relating to the topic (as is possible within the limits of the exam time).
- To be able to show that you have systematically revised the relevant course materials and have understood them well.
- A reasonably well-structured and logical argument (as is possible within the constraints of the exam condition – there is little or no time for redrafting).
- To be able to make clear, relevant and important points that will gain you marks.
- Clarity and conciseness in expression of ideas, concepts, arguments and so on.
- Legibility of handwriting.

Taking essay-type exams

Essay-type exams, just like other types of exams, demand a quick response. It is also important that the answers you produce are accurately directed to the terms of the set questions. Keep the following points and strategies in mind.

- *If there are alternatives, be decisive in selecting the question(s) you will answer*

  It is a waste of valuable time to oscillate from one question to another, or to write plans for all alternative questions first before deciding which one you will answer. The time you waste on indecisiveness can be more effectively used in producing better, well-thought out and well-structured answers.

- *Make sure you understand the questions you will answer*

  Look closely at the wording of each question and make sure you have understood the content you must cover and the way in which you are directed to use it.

- *Plan each of your answers first (on the exam paper itself) before you start writing*

  Jot down points, facts, names, dates and other relevant information, then quickly organise and structure these. Planning is quite important in essay-type exams because you only get to write one draft. This means that before you start writing you need to be reasonably clear on the points you will make, the direction of your argument and so on. (Note however that planning needs to be done quickly, not in a take-all-the-time-in-the-world fashion.)

- *For the structure of the essay, follow the structure of the question*

  So for example, if the question asks you to 'Discuss … then evaluate …', make sure that the first section of your essay focuses on a discussion of the relevant points and issues, and the second section deals with the evaluation (of whatever the question asks you to evaluate).

- *Leave at least a half of a page at the end of each essay you write*

  This is in case you remember something else later that you would want to add to your answer.

- *Try to leave yourself a little time at the end to quickly reread and check the answers you have written*

  Check your essay with regard to clarity, correctness and accuracy of facts (make sure you have written what you really intended to write!) and check your legibility.